Bullying

There was a time when bullying was regarded as a relatively innocuous issue—a normal part of growing up—but this is no longer the case. The magnitude of the problems that bullying can lead to is evidenced by the rising amount of professional literature on bullying, as well as recent cases of bully-linked suicide and homicide in the popular media. Bullying always involves at least one bully and one victim, but there are a variety of social roles that can affect the duration and magnitude of bullying. These roles include bully assistants or supporters, victim defenders, and passive bystanders. Fundamental to creating successful intervention programs to prevent or reduce bullying is basic research that identifies the characteristics of those involved in bullying situations (e.g., personality, motivational, intellectual, physical, social, and behavioural).

This volume presents a broad range of original research describing how social influences are related to bullying. Reflecting the fact that bullying is a world-wide phenomenon and problem, the research comes from samples of individuals from Australia, Finland, Italy, New England, and Poland, as well as a review of the cyber-bullying literature, which is international in scope. This book was originally published as a special issue of *Social Influence.*

Paul R. Nail is a Professor at the University of Central Arkansas, Conway, AR, USA. He holds a Ph.D. in experimental psychology from Texas Christian University, Fort Worth, TX, USA. Besides bullying, his research interests include social influence in groups, cognitive dissonance theory, contemporary theories of racism, political psychology, and individual differences in psychological defenses.

Joan B. Simon is an Associate Professor at the University of Central Arkansas, Conway, AR, USA. Her Ph.D. in school psychology is from the University of Kansas, Lawrence, KS, USA. She is a licensed psychologist whose work on behalf of children with severe emotional needs has been disseminated through professional presentations and publications.

Bullying

A social influence perspective

Edited by
Paul R. Nail and Joan B. Simon

Routledge
Taylor & Francis Group
LONDON AND NEW YORK

First published 2016
by Routledge

2 Park Square, Milton Park, Abingdon, Oxon OX14 4RN
711 Third Avenue, New York, NY 10017, USA

Routledge is an imprint of the Taylor & Francis Group, an informa business

First issued in paperback 2017

British Library Cataloguing in Publication Data
A catalogue record for this book is available from the British Library

ISBN13: 978-1-138-93728-4 (hbk)
ISBN13: 978-1-138-08637-1 (pbk)

Typeset in Times New Roman
by RefineCatch Limited, Bungay, Suffolk

Publisher's Note
The publisher accepts responsibility for any inconsistencies that may have arisen during the conversion of this book from journal articles to book chapters, namely the possible inclusion of journal terminology.

Contents

Citation Information

The chapters in this book were originally published in *Social Influence*, volume 8, issues 2–3 (April–July 2013). When citing this material, please use the original page numbering for each article, as follows:

Chapter 1: Introduction
Introduction to special issue on bullying: A social influence perspective
Joan B. Simon and Paul R. Nail
Social Influence, volume 8, issues 2–3 (April–July 2013) pp. 81–86

Chapter 2
Sticks and stones may break your bones, but words will always hurt you: A review of cyberbullying
V. Skye Wingate, Jessy A. Minney, and Rosanna E. Guadagno
Social Influence, volume 8, issues 2–3 (April–July 2013) pp. 87–106

Chapter 3
Developmental trajectories of adolescent victimization: Predictors and outcomes
Leanne Lester, Donna Cross, Julian Dooley, and Thérèse Shaw
Social Influence, volume 8, issues 2–3 (April–July 2013) pp. 107–130

Chapter 4
Does bullying increase compliance?
Malgorzata Gamian-Wilk
Social Influence, volume 8, issues 2–3 (April–July 2013) pp. 131–148

Chapter 5
Bullying the bully: Why zero-tolerance policies get a failing grade
K. Borgwald and H. Theixos
Social Influence, volume 8, issues 2–3 (April–July 2013) pp. 149–160

Chapter 6

Friend similarity in attitudes toward bullying and sense of responsibility to intervene
Tiziana Pozzoli and Gianluca Gini
Social Influence, volume 8, issues 2–3 (April–July 2013) pp. 161–176

Chapter 7

Overt and relational victimization and adolescent friendships: Selection, de-selection, and social influence
Jelle J. Sijtsema, Ashwin J. Rambaran, and Tiina J. Ojanen
Social Influence, volume 8, issues 2–3 (April–July 2013) pp. 177–195

Chapter 8

Social context of bullying: Do misperceptions of group norms influence children's responses to witnessed episodes?
Marlene Sandstrom, Heather Makover, and Maria Bartini
Social Influence, volume 8, issues 2–3 (April–July 2013) pp. 196–215

Notes on Contributors

Maria Bartini is based in the Department of Psychology at Massachusetts College of Liberal Arts, North Adams, Massachusetts, USA.

K. Borgwald is based in the Philosophy Department at Miami Dade College, Miami, Florida, USA.

Donna Cross is based in the Child Health Promotion Research Centre at Edith Cowan University, Mt. Lawley, Australia.

Julian Dooley is based in the Sellenger Centre for Research in Law, Justice and Social Change at Edith Cowan University, Mt. Lawley, Australia.

Malgorzata Gamian-Wilk is based in the Department of Pedagogies, Psychology Division at the University of Lower Silesia, Wroclaw, Poland.

Gianluca Gini is based in the Department of Developmental and Social Psychology at the University of Padua, Italy.

Rosanna E. Guadagno is based at the National Science Foundation, Division of Cognitive and Behavioral Sciences, Arlington, Virginia, USA.

Leanne Lester is based in the Child Health Promotion Research Centre at Edith Cowan University, Mt. Lawley, Australia.

Heather Makover is based in the Department of Psychology at Williams College, Williamstown, Massachusetts, USA.

Jessy A. Minney is based in the Psychology Department at the University of Alabama, Tuscaloosa, Alabama, USA.

Paul R. Nail is a Professor at the University of Central Arkansas, Conway, AR, USA. He holds a Ph.D. in experimental psychology from Texas Christian University, Fort Worth, TX, USA. Besides bullying, his research interests include social influence in groups, cognitive dissonance theory, contemporary theories of racism, political psychology, and individual differences in psychological defenses.

Tiina J. Ojanen is based in the Department of Psychology at the University of South Florida, Tampa, Florida, USA.

Tiziana Pozzoli is based in the Department of Developmental and Social Psychology at the University of Padua, Italy.

Ashwin J. Rambaran is based in the Department of Sociology at the University of Groningen, The Netherlands.

Marlene Sandstrom is based in the Department of Psychology at Williams College, Williamstown, Massachusetts, USA.

Thérèse Shaw is based in the Child Health Promotion Research Centre at Edith Cowan University, Mt. Lawley, Australia.

Jelle J. Sijtsema is based in the Department of Developmental Psychology at Tilburg University, The Netherlands.

Joan B. Simon is an Associate Professor at the University of Central Arkansas, Conway, AR, USA. Her Ph.D. in school psychology is from the University of Kansas, Lawrence, KS, USA. She is a licensed psychologist whose work on behalf of children with severe emotional needs has been disseminated through professional presentations and publications.

H. Theixos is based in the Philosophy Department at the University of Miami, Coral Gables, Florida, USA.

V. Skye Wingate is based in the Department of Psychology at Morehead State University, Morehead, Kentucky, USA.

Introduction: A social influence perspective

Joan B. Simon and Paul R. Nail
Department of Psychology and Counseling, University of Central Arkansas, Conway, AR, USA

Bullying is a complex social phenomenon that crosses age, ethnicity, and national boundaries. Originally coined as "mobbing," by Olweus in 1972 (Espelage & Swearer, 2003), bullying tends to involve a bully, a victim, and other individuals in a variety of roles that can take the form of an active presence (e.g., bully assistant or victim defender), a passive presence (e.g., bystander), or even a perceived presence (e.g., peer attitudes). Interestingly, these roles tend to be dynamic in that it is not uncommon for an individual to take on different roles from one situation to the next (Espelage & Swearer, 2003). Research on bullying during the past 40 years has provided considerable insight into this phenomenon, but many questions still remain about how we identify bullying, the consequences of such behavior on those involved, and the most effective means to reduce bullying. This special issue of *Social Influence*, dedicated to bullying, responds to some of these unknowns by including a broad range of conceptual and empirical articles describing how social influences are related to the attitudes and/or behaviors of those who take on various roles in a bullying situation.

Traditionally, school-age bullying has been defined by three components: (1) the repeated occurrence of verbal, relational, and/or physical harm by a bully, (2) who is perceived as higher in power than the victim, with (3) the intent to cause harm to the victim (Olweus, 1993; Shore, 2009). The occurrence of bullying has no geographical bounds, as both research and intervention efforts have been seen worldwide (Espelage & Swearer, 2003; Merrell, Gueldner, Ross, & Isava, 2008; Rigby, 2002). The articles in this special issue mirror such efforts, as they include samples of children from Australia, Finland, Italy, New England, and Poland. Estimates from numerous countries indicate that bullies constitute up to 24% of the school-age population and victims up to 44% (Haynie et al., 2001; Nansel et al., 2001; Pellegrini, Bartini, & Brooks, 1999). Bullying tends to increase in frequency during periods of transition, such as the early adolescent transition from elementary to middle school (Espelage & Holt, 2001; Graham, Bellmore, & Mize, 2006; Haynie et al., 2001; Leadbeater, 2010). There is also evidence suggesting that boys are more likely to bully using physical means and less likely to defend a victim than are girls (Haynie et al., 2001; Pellegrini et al., 1999; Salmivalli, Kaukiainen, Kaistaniemi, & Lagerspetz, 1999).

With advances in technology, our understanding of what constitutes bullying is changing (Walker, 2010). Traditionally, bullying was something that occurred away from home, and for victims, the home setting was a safe retreat after the events of the day. There are now many ways (e.g., Internet, smart phones, and social media outlets) by which bullying can occur at any time and in any place. The current article by Wingate, Minney, and Guadagno (2013) compares the components of face-to-face bullying to online cyberbullying. For example, cyberbullying occurs without the visual cues regarding one's intent that are present in a face-to-face bullying situation. Also, cyberbullying includes a greater sense of permanence of a bully's remarks, and subsequent re-victimization, due to their constant presence online or on one's phone.

Regardless of how bullying is formally defined, those victimized by bullies are at greater risk for negative short- and long-term outcomes than are other students. There is an abundance of research demonstrating the links between bullying victimization, and sometimes being a bully as well, and mental health problems such as depression, anxiety, psychosomatic complaints, and suicidal ideation (e.g., Espelage & Holt, 2001; Graham et al., 2006). Two articles in this issue focus on the effects of bullying. The first article by Lester, Cross, Dooley, and Shaw (2013) provides a review of outcome research and presents new longitudinal data from a large group of middle school students in Australia. Some of their findings supported previous research in terms of the outcomes of depression and anxiety in many victims. However, these researchers were surprised to find that depression and anxiety outcomes were more greatly affected by victimization onset at the start of secondary school than by prolonged victimization prior to that time. These results support the need for interventions to reduce bullying at both the elementary/primary and secondary levels.

The second article by Gamian-Wilk (2013) is the one of the article in this issue that focuses on bullying in adulthood versus childhood or adolescence. In this two-study article, the author examined the relationship between being a victim of bullying in the workplace and compliance with coworkers' requests. The first study showed a negative correlation between the two variables, and the second study demonstrated a causal relationship between the two variables when participants were asked to recall a time in which they were socially ostracized at work and then respond to compliance requests. Those participants who were considered victims showed decreased compliance with requests, while interestingly, those participants who were considered non-victims tended to increase requests for compliance after evoking the instance of social ostracism at work. Gamian-Wilk discusses how reduced compliance with requests by those with a history of victimization has the potential to lead to further ostracism in the workplace.

Bullies are also considered at-risk for negative short- and long-term outcomes (Nansel et al., 2001). In this issue, Borgwald and Theixos (2013) explore the mental health outcomes (e.g., stress, depression, and drug use) for bullies who are expelled from school as a result of their actions. They present a perspective that current anti-bullying policies, which use expulsion as the consequence for bullying, are ineffective, unjust, and implemented in socially biased ways. Alternatively, they propose improved efforts to educate those who bully, provide empathy training to enhance social skills, and allow opportunities for apologies and forgiveness between the bully and victim.

If bullying were simply a social interaction between one bully and one victim, it would be easier to understand the dynamics of the dyad interaction and intervene accordingly. Unfortunately, bullying usually occurs within a broader social content and both influences and is influenced by the attitudes and behaviors of others. It is for this reason that most anti-bullying programs are systemic in nature, i.e., they include individual, school, family, and community components (Merrell et al., 2008; Smith, Schneider, Smith, & Ananiadou, 2004; Ttofi & Farrington, 2011). There are two studies in this issue that address bullying-related characteristics of friend dyads and friendship selection.

Pozzoli and Gini (2013) examined homophily, the degree to which "social interactions occur more frequently among similar individuals than among dissimilar individuals" (p. 163). They found that mutually nominated friends were more similar in their attitudes toward bullying and their sense of responsibility for intervening in bullying situations than were non-friends; furthermore, the more reciprocal friends a child had, the better friends' sense of responsibility predicted the individual's sense of responsibility. They also observed that girls held more negative attitudes toward bullying than did boys.

Sijtsema, Rambaran, and Ojanen (2013) explored friendship selection and de-selection over time among a group of middle school students and their relation to self-reported victimization through relational (e.g., teasing, calling names, and rumors) or overt (e.g., direct verbal or physical attacks) means. Results from this study also demonstrated homophily in that students who were high on relational victimization were more likely to extend friendship nominations than those who were also high on relational victimization. This trend was not present for students who experienced overt victimization; however, students did grow more similar to their reciprocal friends over time in terms of their self-reported overt victimization.

Although the two previous studies examined similarities between friends in terms of attitudes and victimization, the current study by Sandstrom, Makover, and Bartini (2013) explored how perceived group norms influence children's joining the bully or defending the victim behaviors in a bullying situation.

Overall, children's self-reported pro-social attitudes were considered to be higher than their estimates of peers' attitudes. Furthermore, the children who underestimated peers' pro-social attitudes were more likely to join the bully, whereas those who overestimated peers' pro-social attitudes were more likely to defend the victim. Taken together, these three studies demonstrate some of the similarities and differences between children and their peers in the context of a bullying situation.

There has been an abundance of research on bullying during the past 30 years (Hansen, Steenberg, Palic, & Elklit, 2012; Jordan & Austin, 2012; Salmivalli, 2010; Ttofi & Farrington, 2011). In fact, this special issue is one of many in both US and international journals that have addressed the topic of bullying during the school-age years (e.g., Elias & Zins (Eds.), *School Psychology International*, 2003; Geffner & Loring (Eds.), *Journal of Emotional Abuse*, 2001; Leff & Crick (Eds.), *School Psychology Review*, 2010; Smith & Brian (Eds.), *Aggressive Behavior*, 2000). In spite of such abundant efforts, there is still much to learn about it. For example, there is little known about how ethnicity/race, sexual orientation, or religious affiliation influences the occurrence of bullying or the ways in which bullying is viewed by individuals or the social group as a whole. Also, our understanding of why seemingly well-adjusted children sometimes bully is limited. For example, why do students who report having good friends, high self-esteem, and few mental health difficulties bully others? There is some research that gives insight into personality dynamics of bullies and the factors that drive them to behave this way (Nail, Bihm, & Simon, in press; Salmivalli et al., 1999). Lastly, there have been only a few efforts to understand which components of anti-bullying programs are most effective and why (Merrell et al., 2008; Smith et al., 2004; Ttofi & Farrington, 2011).

In conclusion, bullying is a complex social phenomenon in which a victim(s) is intentionally harmed, belittled, intimidated, and so on, through physical, verbal, or written means. Our best efforts, through anti-bullying laws and policies (National Center for Mental Health Promotion and Youth Violence Prevention, 2011) and/or systematic universal or selected intervention (Merrell et al., 2008; Smith et al., 2004), have failed to consistently demonstrate positive outcomes that lead to significant reductions in bullying behavior. Therefore, researchers must persist in their efforts to better understand why bullying occurs so that those working to prevent bullying or intervene when it occurs can be more targeted in their approach. The articles in this special issue of *Social Influence* bring us one step closer to this desired end.

REFERENCES

Borgwald, K., & Theixos, H. (2013). Bullying the bully: Why zero-tolerance policies get a failing grade. *Social Influence*, *8*, 149–160.

Espelage, D. L., & Holt, M. K. (2001). Bullying and victimization during early adolescence: Peer influences and psychosocial correlates. *Journal of Emotional Abuse, 2*, 123–142.

Espelage, D. L., & Swearer, S. M. (2003). Research on school bullying and victimization: What we have learned and where do we go from here? *School Psychology Review, 32*, 365–383.

Gamian-Wilk, M. (2013). Does bullying increase compliance? *Social Influence, 8*, 131–148.

Graham, S., Bellmore, A. D., & Mize, J. (2006). Peer victimization, aggression, and their co-occurrence in middle school: Pathways to adjustment problems. *Journal of Abnormal Child Psychology, 34*, 363–378.

Hansen, T., Steenberg, L., Palic, S., & Elklit, A. (2012). A review of psychological factors related to bullying victimization in schools. *Aggression and Violent Behavior, 17*, 383–387.

Haynie, D. L., Nansel, T., Eitel, P., Crump, A. D., Saylor, K., Yu, K., & Simons-Morton, B. (2001). Bullies, victims, and bully/victims: Distinct groups of at-risk youth. *Journal of Early Adolescence, 21*, 29–49.

Jordan, K., & Austin, J. (2012). A review of the literature on bullying in U.S. schools and how a parent-educator partnership can be an effective way to handle bullying. *Journal of Aggression, Maltreatment, & Trauma, 21*, 440–458.

Leadbeater, B. (2010). Can we see it? Can we stop it? Lessons learned from community-university research collaborations about relational aggression. *School Psychology Review, 39*, 588–593.

Lester, L., Cross, D., Dooley, J., & Shaw, T. (2013). Developmental trajectories of adolescent victimization: Predictors and outcomes. *Social Influence, 8*, 107–130.

Merrell, K. W., Gueldner, B. A., Ross, S. W., & Isava, D. M. (2008). How effective are school bullying intervention programs? A meta-analysis of intervention research. *School Psychology Quarterly, 23*, 26–42.

Nail, P. R., Bihm, E. M., & Simon, J. B. (in press). Is school-yard bullying driven by defensive personality? In T. Patelis (Ed.), *Proceedings of the 5th annual international conference on psychology*. Athens, Greece: Athens Institute for Education and Research.

Nansel, T. R., Overpeck, M., Pilla, R. S., Ruan, W. J., Simons-Morton, B., & Scheidt, P. (2001). Bullying behaviors among US youth: Prevalence and association with psychosocial adjustment. *Journal of the American Medical Association, 285*, 2094–2100.

National Center for Mental Health Promotion and Youth Violence Prevention (2011). *Bullying prevention state laws*. Retrieved from http://www.promoteprevent.org/publications/prevention-briefs/bullying-prevention-state-laws

Olweus, D. (1993). *Bullying at school*. Malden, MA: Blackwell Publishing.

Pellegrini, A. D., Bartini, M., & Brooks, F. (1999). School bullies, victims, and aggressive victims: Factors relating to group affiliation and victimization in early adolescence. *Journal of Educational Psychology, 91*, 216–224.

Pozzoli, T., & Gini, G. (2013). Friend similarity in attitudes toward bullying and sense of responsibility to intervene. *Social Influence, 8*, 161–176.

Rigby, K. (2002). *A meta-evaluation of methods and approaches to reducing bullying in pre-schools and in early primary school in Australia*. Retrieved from http://www.kenrigby.net/meta.pdf

Salmivalli, C. (2010). Bullying and the peer group: A review. *Aggression and Violent Behavior*, *15*, 112–120.

Salmivalli, C., Kaukiainen, A., Kaistaniemi, L., & Lagerspetz, K. (1999). Self-evaluated self-esteem, peer-evaluated self-esteem, and defensive egotism as predictors of adolescents' participation in bullying situations. *Personality and Social Psychology Bulletin*, *25*, 1268–1278.

Sandstrom, M., Makover, H., & Bartini, M. (2013). Social context of bullying: Do misperceptions of group norms influence children's responses to witnessed episodes? *Social Influence*, *8*, 196–215.

Shore, K. (2009). Preventing bullying: Nine ways to bully-proof your classroom. *The Education Digest*, *75*, 39–44.

Sijtsema, J. J., Rambaran, A. J., & Ojanen, T. J. (2013). Overt and relational victimization and adolescent friendships: Selection, de-selection, and social influence. *Social Influence*, *8*, 177–195.

Smith, J. D., Schneider, B. H., Smith, P. K., & Ananiadou, K. (2004). The effectiveness of whole-school antibullying programs: A synthesis of evaluation research. *School Psychology Review*, *33*, 547–560.

Ttofi, M. M., & Farrington, D. P. (2011). Effectiveness of school-based programs to reduce bullying: A systematic and meta-analytic review. *Journal of Experimental Criminology*, *7*, 27–56.

Walker, H. M. (2010). Relational aggression in schools: Implications for future research on screening intervention and prevention. *School Psychology Review*, *39*, 594–600.

Wingate, V. S., Minney, J. A., & Guadagno, R. E. (2013). Sticks and stones may break your bones, but words will always hurt you: A review of cyberbullying. *Social Influence*, *8*, 87–106.

Sticks and stones may break your bones, but words will always hurt you: A review of cyberbullying

V. Skye Wingate[1], Jessy A. Minney[2], and Rosanna E. Guadagno[3]
[1]Department of Psychology, Morehead State University, Morehead, KY, USA
[2]Psychology Department, The University of Alabama, Tuscaloosa, AL, USA
[3]National Science Foundation, Division of Cognitive and Behavioral Sciences, Arlington, VA, USA

In this paper we review the bullying literature, comparing and contrasting traditional face-to-face bullying and online "cyberbullying". More specifically we deconstruct the current working definitions of both types of bullying and compare the plethora of operational definitions. We explore characteristics of online environments and how these attributes facilitate and accentuate online bullying, while portraying the impact this type of bullying may have on victims as a result of this environment. Next we differentiate between reactive and proactive aggression and how certain bullying techniques are categorized. Finally we examine conflicting data regarding gender differences in cyberbullying roles, discuss parental monitoring, and investigate activism and intervention.

For many teenagers high school is a difficult period of adjustment, fraught with the tension of navigating an increasingly complicated social world and developing an identity independent from one's parents. For teenagers like Jamey Rodemeyer, the anxiety and awkwardness of adolescence was compounded by daily torment from his peers for self-identifying as gay.

The authors would like to thank Mary Margaret Popova for her insightful comments and thoughtful editing on earlier versions of this manuscript, and Wesley Burge for his help in compiling references.

Jamey, who lived in a suburb near Buffalo, New York, experienced daily bullying at school, and nightly bullying online. His peers routinely posted vicious comments about him on social networking sites, which were then publicly visible. In September 2011, Jamey—only 14 years old—committed suicide. He left indications that the chronic online torment he endured contributed to his tragic decision to take his own life. Unfortunately Jamey is far from the only victim of cyberbullying, but his story illustrates that cyberbullying must be taken seriously. What can be learned from this tragedy? The stories of Jamey, and others similar to him, highlight the need for an empirical understanding of how cyberbullying differs from traditional bullying, and how the perpetrators affect their victims in online environments. This level of understanding will hopefully aid in the development of effective interventions to combat cyberbullying and protect the victims of cyberbullying.

DEFINING CYBERBULLYING

The schoolyard used to have a monopoly on bullying, but not anymore. Children who were bullied in school and on the playground could retreat to the safety of their homes and escape the jeers and taunts of their peers. The Internet, through social networking, instant messaging, text messaging, and email, has brought bullying into the home and made it virtually ubiquitous for today's wired teens. Traditionally bullying has been conceptualized as having three key elements: (1) the perpetrator must intend to cause harm to the victim, (2) the behavior must be repeated and chronic in nature, and (3) and there must be some power differential between the victim and the perpetrator (Solberg & Olweus, 2003). This definition of bullying encompasses a wide range of aggressive behaviors, and can be primarily verbal, relational, physical, or a combination of these behaviors (Wang, Iannotti, & Nansel, 2009).

The cyberbullying literature has suffered from the absence of a "gold standard" definition. A review of recent literature on cyberbullying revealed that researchers have varied significantly in their definitions in terms of which elements of traditional bullying are included in their operational definitions (Dooley, Pyzalski, & Cross, 2009; Kowalski, Limber, & Agatston, 2008). Li (2008, p.224) simply defines cyberbullying as "bullying via electronic communication tools," which implies that all three elements (intent, chronicity, and power differential) must be present for the behavior to be considered cyberbullying. In contrast to this broad, and somewhat amorphous, definition, Willard (2007, p.1) offers this definition: "Sending or posting harmful or cruel texts or images using the Internet or other digital communication devices." This definition seems overly narrow, and does not allow for the rapidly changing nature of technology. Smith and colleagues

(2008, p. 376) use a definition that most closely aligns cyberbullying with its traditional, face-to-face counterpart: "An aggressive, intentional act carried out by a group or individual, using electronic forms of contact, repeatedly or over time against a victim who cannot easily defend him or herself." This definition includes all three of the primary elements of face-to-face bullying. However, to adequately define cyberbullying, it is important to consider how cyberbullying may differ in these three aspects from traditional cyberbullying. How does the nature of electronic or computer-mediated communication change the dynamics between the perpetrator and the victim? We propose that the power differential between the perpetrator and the victim becomes immaterial due to the properties of computer-mediated communication (CMC). Patchin and Hinduja (2006, p. 152) similarly employed a definition that does not require a power differential in order for a behavior to be considered cyberbullying: "Willful and repeated harm inflicted through the medium of electronic text." This contends that the intent and chronicity are central to cyberbullying; however, recent research has shown that only 5% of the perpetrators of cyberbullying admitted malicious intent (Law, Shapka, Domene, & Gagne, 2012). The remaining 95% contended that their behavior was harmless teasing. However, the stories of Jamey and others like him belie the harmlessness of the behavior. It is noteworthy that the perpetrators do not ascribe malice to their actions when they engage in cyberbullying, and this is not the case for those who engage in face-to-face bullying (Erdur-Baker, 2010). Thus, in cyberbullying literature, the definitions vary widely, as do the corresponding operational definitions.

Although there has been some disagreement on operational definitions (i.e., what behaviors should be considered cyberbullying; Tokunaga, 2010), and in defining the concept owing to the variation in methods (Kowalski et al., 2008); for the sake of consistency we will adopt the definition postulated by Dooley et al. (2009) which identifies cyberbullying as the intentional and habitual use of fear or humiliation to intimidate a victim and demonstrate superiority over electronic mediums. Regardless of conceptual or operational definition, it is unambiguously clear that cyberbullying has the potential to cause serious psychological harm to victims.

The fact that not everyone will agree with what does, and does not, constitute cyberbullying is also a point of discussion. For instance, in a recent cross-cultural study spanning six European countries, this definitional discrepancy is clearly manifested Menesini et al. systematically manipulated the three criteria of traditional bullying (intentionality, repetition, and imbalance of power) while presenting two new cyberbullying criteria (public vs private/anonymous) to examine empirically what the adolescents consider cyberbullying. After evaluating the cyberbullying scenarios, most of the adolescents sampled ($N = 2257$) considered the traditional bullying criteria applicable to cyberbullying, with the notable exception of repetition. The authors argue that repetition is not as relevant in virtual environments because the nature of information and communication technology allows opportunity for multiple victimizations without repeated contribution from any one perpetrator (Menesini & Spiel, 2012). They also found the most meaningful criterion for defining cyberbullying was imbalance of power; this outweighed intentionality and anonymity in relevance. The strength of the imbalance of power criterion replicated across six countries (Italy, Spain, Germany, Estonia, Sweden and France) and encompassed all types of behavior (Menesini et al., 2012).

In the present review we explore how computer-mediated communication changes the nature of bullying interactions. We will also investigate the forms and potential causes of aggression, and the ways in which victims and perpetrators of cyberbullying differ. We also investigate environmental considerations, gender differences in cyberbullying roles, and cyberbullying interventions.

AGGRESSION AS A COMPONENT OF CYBERBULLYING

Aggression is primarily defined by two different dimensions. The first dimension reflects the type of behaviors: direct (overt/physical) vs relational (covert/social). The second dimension reflects the intent of the perpetrator: proactive (goal oriented and intentional) vs reactive (response to a perceived provocation). Cyberbullying can be direct or relational, and it can be either proactive or reactive; it can manifest in many different ways.

Direct vs relational aggression

Bullying is one of several types of aggressive behaviors. Two evenly matched children fighting on the playground would be considered aggression, but not be considered bullying, while an older child repeatedly stealing the lunch money of a younger child through threats and intimidation is certainly aggression and bullying. The example of the lunch money meets all three traditional bullying criteria: the older child has an age and presumably size advantage (power differential), the behavior occurs daily (chronicity), and the older child intends to harm the younger child by depriving him of lunch (intent). This type of bullying is considered direct, or overt, aggression which refers to physical acts of intimidation or displaying aggressive mannerisms to assert power over another (Olweus, 1991; Pellegrini & Bartini, 2001; Smith & Boulton, 1990). Like most other types of direct aggression, boys are much more likely to engage in directly aggressive types of bullying behaviors (Bjorkqvist, 1994; Goldbaum, Craig, Pepler, & Connolly, 2007; Owens, Shute, & Slee, 2007; Wang et al., 2009).

Conversely, relational aggression manifests itself in a subtler manner. It encompasses rumors, gossip, and non-physical personal attacks (Bosworth, Espelage, & Simon, 1999; Underwood, Galen, & Paquette, 2001). Relational aggression (Crick & Grotpeter, 1995) can also extend to include behaviors such as sending harassing text messages, posting hurtful comments on a social networking site, and spreading embarrassing information such as photos or personal writings (Law, Shapka, Domene, & Gagné, 2012; Smith, Mahdavi, Carvalho, & Tippett, 2006). These behaviors can be considered cyberbullying when the perpetrator routinely targets the same victim. Relational aggression typically involves a power differential within the social hierarchy, rather than a power differential based on physical characteristics. Research shows that girls are more likely to engage in relational, rather than direct, types of bullying (Coyne, Archer, & Eslea, 2006; Wang et al., 2009). Girls are also more likely to be cyberbullied by text messaging and mobile phone calls, which are more relational forms of cyberbullying (Smith et al., 2006). However, although girls tend to engage in relational bullying at a higher frequency than direct bullying, boys have been found to engage in relational aggression at the same frequency as girls (Crampanzano, Frick, & Terranova, 2010). This has been shown to be true offline.

Reactive vs proactive aggression

What is the motivation for perpetrators to engage in cyberbullying? The current section examines two motivations for bullying: reactive and proactive aggression. Reactive aggression is the perpetrator's response to an actual or perceived provocation, while proactive aggression is deliberately instigated by the perpetrator for the purpose of obtaining resources or achieving goals (Crick & Dodge, 1996; Dodge & Coie, 1987) ranging from providing humor or entertainment to the bully to extorting personal information (Law et al., 2012). Reactive aggression is associated with hostile attribution of intent within ambiguous social environments (e.g., Crick & Dodge, 1996; Hartman & Stage, 2000; Orobio de Castro, Veerman, Koops, Bosch, & Monshouwer, 2002). Because cyberspace lacks physical cues and other social prompts, communicating via the Internet could be considered an ambiguous context, and therefore communicators may attribute hostile intent to neutral stimuli. This "tit for tat" aggression can begin and maintain the cycle of cyberbullying.

Traditional bullying behaviors can be either reactive or proactive, and that determination is often murky. Cyberbullying behaviors, which would typically be considered reactive aggression include: sharing private messages with unintended recipients or making embarrassing pictures public (Law et al., 2012). Proactive cyberbullying behavior would include creating hostile websites solely for the purpose of harming another person, or manufacturing a fake online persona to extract potentially damaging information from a victim (Law et al., 2012).

Recent research shows cyberbullying is more likely to result from proactive aggression than reactive (Calvete, Orue, Estevez, Villardon, & Padilla, 2010). Calvete et al. also assert that, in comparison to other violent behaviors in adolescents, cyberbullying should be categorized as proactive and indirect aggression. This assertion is supported by previous literature on traditional bullying where it was also shown to be most closely associated with proactive, rather than reactive, aggression (Roland & Idsøe, 2001; Schwartz et al., 1998; Unnever, 2005). In contrast, indirect aggression (also known as relational aggression), involving the manipulation of relationships in order to harm others (Bjorkqvist, 2001; Bjorkqvist, Lagerspetz, & Kaukiainen, 1992; Crick & Grotpeter, 1995), is also utilized in various cyberbullying situations where a person is isolated from the peer group and relationships are intentionally broken (Crick, 1995; Galen & Underwood, 1997). When cyberbullying behaviors are framed in this way, it can also be argued that cyberbullying displays traditional indirect bullying characteristics as well (Dehue, Bolman, & Vollink, 2008) thereby defining cyberbullying as a type of indirect or relational aggression (Piazza & Bering, 2009).

FACE-TO-FACE COMMUNICATION VS COMPUTER-MEDIATED COMMUNICATION

Online environments reduce the salience of interaction with other people, while increasing the amount of perceived anonymity (McKenna & Bargh, 2000). This anonymity provides a sense of protection to communicators and may empower them into saying things they normally would not in a face-to-face context (Peter, Valkenburg, & Schouten, 2005; Ward & Tracey, 2004). Due to the anonymity and group salience elicited by Internet communication, depersonalization and deindividuation are also heightened (Postmes, Spears, & Lea, 2002). As a result, group salience and polarization increase. This group mentality facilitates behavior that might not be acceptable to individuals if the communication circumstances were different (e.g., face-to-face). Therefore online communicators accept group norms rather than adhering to individual standards of behavior (Postmes et al., 2002). If the individuals engaging in online interaction feel anonymous, they are not thinking about the repercussions of their behaviors online, and are not feeling any uncomfortable tension regarding their Internet expression, then they will most likely continue that normative group behavior. This would suggest that the bullying in cyberspace is perpetuated by the environment itself, and its unique characteristics exacerbate the prevalence of cyberbullying.

Owing to the deindividuation and salience of group norms online, we suggest cyberbullying displays components of a mob mentality. Canning (2010) asserts that although it is easy to evaluate one person's willful harm to another as a reflection of a deviant individual, the same does not hold true for group indiscretions. Instead Canning suggests that it is not as easy to assign a delinquent personality to every individual in the group; thus it is difficult to dismiss the collective behavior on deviant personalities (Canning, 2010). We can therefore conclude there may be ambiguous reasons for the engagement of virtual bullying; and because of the sense of online conformity and unification there, as in a mob, is a clouding of responsibility and motive.

One of the most pertinent components of online bullying is the lack of nonverbal cues. Physical attractiveness and facial expression are among the physical cues that are not salient in online situations, due to the nature of the interaction (Amichai-Hamburger & McKenna, 2006; Morton, Zettelmeyer, & Silva-Risso, 2003). However, when examining cyberbullying, the absence of nonverbal cues seems to exaggerate the bullying itself. Message salience is increased because attention is focused on the text and not diluted by extraneous visual stimuli such as the communicator (Guadagno & Cialdini, 2002). Therefore the perpetrator cannot see the victim's facial expression and cannot see the reaction when the words are being read. Research supports the notion that these visual cues impact the reception and interpretation of online information (Epley & Kruger, 2005).

Furthermore the absence of proximity to a cyberbully does not necessarily reduce the impact of a message on the target. McKenna and Bargh (2000) argue that proximity can be social, as well as physical. Individuals in shared online environments, such as chat rooms or strings of email conversations, may perceive social closeness to those with whom they are communicating remotely. The facilitated social intimacy of certain types of online communication can result in interactions that more closely resemble face-to-face encounters. As it relates to cyberbullying, the feeling of social proximity may negate any message dilution resulting from physical distance.

Face-to-face communication and computer-mediated communication also differ in the time and pace of the interaction. During an online interaction the sender can relay a message without knowing or considering the recipient's schedule. Furthermore there is a greater amount of time and control across the interaction (McKenna & Bargh, 2000). Having diminished time limitations, options like retyping messages and logging off an online site allow for a more methodical means of communication. This type of communication can be highly controlled and intentional. Due to the deliberate nature of this communication, messages may be perceived as more calculated and representative of the speaker's intentions. Most importantly, the message recipient has the opportunity to repeatedly reread any messages that have been sent. The sense of permanence elicited from the communication mode and the social proximity of the environment may result in the victims of cyberbullying being more severely impacted than victims of face-to-face bullying.

One aspect of computer-mediated communication that has not yet been studied as it relates to cyberbullying is the extent to which it limits the victim's feeling of control in the situation. If an individual is bullied in a face-to-face situation, when s/he recalls the incident later s/he can emphasize or de-emphasize aspects of the interactions selectively. The narrative of the incident can be personally tailored to allow the victim to cope with it psychologically (Bollmer, Milich, Harris, & Maras, 2005). Cyberbullying may be uniquely harmful to victims because the narrative is being provided by the bully. This feeling could produce learned helplessness, which may contribute to the higher rates of depression among individuals who are victims of cyberbullying (Schenk & Fremouw, 2012). Future research should address how differences in victims' narratives of their face-to-face and cyberbullying experiences predict later psychological adjustment. Overall it seems clear that cyberbullying is uniquely harmful to victims because of the ways in which computer-mediated communication differs from face-to-face communication.

Jamey Rodemeyer used the social networking site Formspring which allows anonymous posts. He was constantly bombarded by public messages comprised of gay slurs, derogatory descriptions of his physical appearance and sexuality, and even suggestions and prompts for him to no longer live. In Jamey's case, and in many others, the avalanche of negative feedback being posted on his networking page became overwhelming.

Unfortunately, with greater accessibility to computers and Internet, the prominence of online aggression may be increasing (Hinduja & Patchin, 2008; Ybarra & Mitchell, 2004a). However, considering the high level of variance regarding cyberbullying rates is likely owing to variability in the measurement and the operational definition (Kowalski et al., 2008), it would be meaningless to compare the prevalence between traditional and cyber acts of bullying. Although cyberbullying may be increasingly rampant, the social responsibility of those participating in these destructive activities is disturbingly low. More specifically, 95% of kids who report they are engaging in cyberbullying activities perceive their behavior as harmless and intended for humor, while a mere 5% actually intended for their behavior to harm the recipient(s) (Shapka et al., 2012). This may suggest that the main motivation for cyberbullying is not rooted in reactive aggression (Crick & Dodge, 1996; Dodge & Coie, 1987) since the bullying is not retaliatory. Therefore cyberbullying may be primarily initiated for the goal of humor and thereby stem from proactive aggression. So, who are these perpetrators of cyberbullying, why do they engage in these behaviors, and how do they differ from those who bully face-to-face?

VICTIMS VS PERPETRATORS

Being the victim of bullying has significant long-term consequences on a child's mental health and emotional well-being (Olweus, 1991, 1994). Children who are bullied perform poorly in school, are less engaged, and are at a significantly higher risk for developing clinical levels of internalizing disorders such an anxiety and depression (e.g., Arseneault et al., 2006; Bacchini, Esposito, & Affuso, 2009; Boivin, Hymel, & Burkowski, 1995; Craig, 1998). Additionally, children who routinely engage in face-to-face bullying, especially direct and proactive aggressive behaviors will often experience negative consequences such as social rejection (Lochman & Wells, 2002).

The subsequent section highlights characteristics which may discriminate between children who engage in face-to-face vs cyber forms of bullying, and addresses the previously raised supposition that girls may be more likely to engage in cyberbullying (Hinduja & Patchin, 2008) since girls also engage in more indirect forms of bullying than do boys (Baldry 1998; Crick 1995; Crick, Casas, & Mosher 1997; Crick & Grotpeter 1995) and indirect types of bullying pervade cyberbulling instances (Hinduja & Patchin, 2008). It is interesting to note that a bully's need for power and notoriety is achieved simply by recruiting others to target the same victim (Shariff, 2009). Although these proactive bullies are displaying destructive behaviors towards another person, proactively aggressive children are viewed as strong leaders with high social status, sense of humor, and positive attributes regarding friendship development and maintenance (Dodge & Coie, 1987). And, as Dooley et al. (2009) summarize, there is definite need for further research regarding several aspects of cyberbullying, which include motivation and power issues, considering there is often a delayed achievement of the cyberbully's goals.

Furthermore a recent exploratory study conducted among Italian adolescents proposed four roles ("pure" bullies, "pure" victims, bully victims, and noninvolved subjects), asked each participant to identify with one role, and examined the moral disengagement, aggression, and empathy of every person (Renati, Berrone, & Zanetti, (2012). Participants who identified themselves as either bullies or victims were higher in moral disengagement and scored higher in both proactive and reactive aggression.

Renati et al. also found that cyberbullies exhibited an absence of affective empathy.

Environmental considerations

There are some environmental characteristics which may contribute to children engaging in cyberbullying. Children who have Internet access in their bedrooms report higher rates of sending hostile messages online, as well as more overall misconduct on the Internet (i.e., lying about their age to access websites or viewing pornographic materials) (Ridout, Roberts, & Foehr, 2005). Parental monitoring refers to a parent's attention to their child's whereabouts, such as setting a curfew, and also includes the extent to which children are left unsupervised (Essau, Sasagawa, & Frick, 2006; Shelton, Frick, & Wootton, 1996). Parental monitoring is related to an increase engagement in cyberbullying (Law, Shapka, & Olson, 2010; Stattin & Kerr, 2000).

Gender differences

In general, males have been shown to engage in more bullying behaviors than females (Forero, McLellan, Rissel, & Baum, 1999; Nansel et al., 2001; Sourander, Helstela, Helenius, & Piha, 2000). However, Blair (2003) and Kimborough, Guadagno, Muscanell, and Dill (2012) both reported that women are more likely to communicate using text messaging and emails than are men. Dooley et al. (2009) draw theoretical conclusions from Blair's work and postulated that because girls use text and emails more than boys, girls may have more opportunities for both victimizing and being victimized online.

Previous research has typically found that, compared to face-to-face bullying, boys are more likely to be physically victimized, and girls are more likely to be relationally victimized (Crick & Dodge, 1996). However, more-current research is less clear on how gender relates to the likelihood of being the victim of cyberbullying. Some studies have found that girls are more likely to be both the victims and perpetrators of cyberbullying (e.g., Smith et al., 2008), while others have found that the perpetrators of both traditional and cyber bullying were more likely to be male (Li, 2006; Slonje & Smith, 2008). These discrepancies could also be the result of a reporting bias; Li (2006) found that female victims of cyberbullying were more likely to report it to an adult.

Walrave and Heirman (2011) found that girls had a higher propensity to become victims of cyberbullying while boys tended to engage in electronic bullying more than girls. In contrast, Slonje and Smith (2008) found boys to be slightly more likely to be cyberbullies. This was the case in all Smith et al. (2006) cyberbullying categories, yet bullying via text messaging was the only type that revealed gender differences. Finally, Ybarra and Mitchell (2004b) found no significant gender differences in either cyber victims or cyber bullies. Thus, overall, the literature on gender differences in cyberbullying indicates that more research needs to be conducted before conclusions can be drawn.

REASONS FOR LACK OF CYBERBULLYING INTERVENTION

Given the severe long-term consequences of bullying, both face-to-face and cyberbullying, why do classmates fail to intervene on behalf of their peers to prevent or minimize it? One possible explanation is pluralistic ignorance—a group-level phenomenon in which all the group members privately hold one opinion on a given topic, but they all maintain their silence because they incorrectly assume the other group members hold the opposite view (Katz, Allport, & Jenness, 1931). A related phenomenon which may also help explain students' reluctance to help their peers is the bystander effect; bullying is often conceptualized as being a triad comprised of bully, victim, and witness (i.e., bystander) (Latane & Darley, 1968). The bystander effect refers to the lack of action by all members of a group while they are witnessing someone in need of assistance. Diffusion of responsibility permeates the situation when each witness feels as if another witness will help the person in need. Unfortunately as the number of people who witness the bullying increases, so does the diffusion of responsibility, and the likelihood of anyone intervening on the behalf of the victims decreases. The greater the diffusion of responsibility the less likely help will actually be given to the victim (Li, 2007). Online, particularly on social networking sites, a cyberbullying target may have hundreds of friends. If they do not react this creates the impression that ignoring the cyberbullying is the normative response. Another factor that may contribute to high prevalence of cyberbullying is that the most common type of cyberbullying is verbal and is considered a "mild" form of bullying (Rivers & Smith, 1994). In fact, this type of bullying is often considered "joking" by the perpetrators (Teräsahjo & Salmivalli, 2003).

Certain individual factors also contribute to whether witnesses of bullying will help the victim. Children who are more likely to help tend to be emotionally stable (Tani, Greenman, Schneider, & Fregoso, 2003), cognitively accelerated (Pozzoli & Gini, 2012), and typically have strong anti-bullying attitudes (Salmivalli & Voeten, 2004). Defenders of victims are also highly empathic (Caravita, Pöyhönen, Rajala, & Salmivalli, 2011; Gini, 2008; Salmivalli & Nieminen, 2002; Salmivalli & Voeten, 2004), possess a strong confidence in being able to defend (Salmivalli & Voeten, 2004; Salmivalli, Voeten, & Poskiparta, 2011), and are usually nominated by their peers as defenders. Research also shows that younger children tend to assist victims more so than older children, and girls are more likely to be nominated as defenders by both peers and the victims (Caravita et al., 2011; Menesini & Nocentini, 2009; Salmivalli & Voeten, 2004; Salmivalli et al., 2011).

ANTI-BULLYING PROGRAMS

Anti-bullying programs are widely implemented in elementary and middle schools, and some programs have recently begun to address cyberbullying as a focus of intervention (Bhat, 2008; Diamanduros, Downs, & Jenkins, 2008). However, recent research found that many teachers do not consider cyberbullying to be a serious threat, and that as many as 25% of teachers feel cyberbullying is actually helpful to children in preparing them for the real world (Stauffer, Heath, Coyne, & Ferrin, 2012). This is cause for serious concern as cyberbullying is not atypical. The effectiveness of anti-bullying programs could be blunted by students' perceptions that teachers do not take cyberbullying seriously. This could also hamper the timely reporting of incidents to faculty members. Strategies to improve teacher understanding of cyberbullying could include in-service trainings at the schools, or even low-intensity interventions such as having designated "safe rooms." Many schools allow faculty to display stickers on their doors to indicate they are safe people for LGBT students to talk to; a similar strategy could be implemented to indicate faculty who are designated to handle bullying and cyberbullying problems.

ACTIVISM TO DECREASE CYBERBULLYING

There are several steps that can be taken in order to reduce the frequency of cyberbullying incidences. According to Campbell (2005) there are four areas that have been shown to reduce traditional bullying in schools that could also be used to suppress the occurrence of cyberbullying: awareness raising, whole school policies, supervision, and programs. The first step to this prevention program is to raise awareness. One of the early problems that may be encountered with programs of this kind is the lack of recognition or acknowledgment of bullying incidences by the school itself (Besag, 1989). School faculty, teachers, parents, and students need to be informed of what bullying behaviors exist and how rampant they can be in this electronic age. Second, the implementation of whole school policies provides consistency when identifying and reprimanding bullying. According to Smith and Sharp (1994), it is the most effective action a school can take in reducing face-to-face bullying.

Third, it is already known that adult supervision greatly decreases face-to-face bullying (Smith & Shu, 2000), and teachers are already aware of the dangers of pornography online and monitor students' computer use carefully (Kerawalla & Crook, 2002). Finally, Campbell (2005) suggests two types of programs to reduce bullying: social programs and curriculum programs. Social programs focus on the bystanders or witnesses of school bullying and attempts to instill empathic reactions in the surrounding peers so bullying does not get ignored or condoned (Noble, 2003). Also, curriculum programs could be utilized to directly teach "netiquette" (appropriate etiquette or behavior online) and empathy through the use of stories that are already part of the teaching material.

Other researchers agree that education is key to preventing bullying from occurring, while also focusing more attention on the legal aspects of cyberbullying (Butler, Kift, & Campbell, 2010). Essentially, students need to be cognizant of the identifiable information and images they are sharing online; however schools also reserve the right to discipline students for behavior occurring off school grounds and beyond school hours, if said behavior negatively affects students' safety and quality of education (Kift, Campbell, & Butler, 2010). A key step to reducing bullying is better educating children as to what behaviors constitute bullying. Children and adults have demonstrated a reluctance to label the behavior of peers, especially friends, as bullying (Mishna, 2004). Future research questions posed by Mishna, Wiener, and Pepler (2008) include identifying the point where conflict becomes bullying, examining the degrees of emotional distress on bullied children, and identifying helpful ways for victims to address bullying behavior.

Overall, one thing is certain: cyberbullying is a problem and it harms those victimized by it. Even though it will probably not be totally extinguished, keeping cyberbullying in school and home discussions can discourage perpetrators and inform victims of possible means of reporting such behavior. But most importantly, let us not forget the message Jamey spread before his death: "I just want to tell you that it does get better. Just love yourself and you're set" – Jamey Rodemeyer.

REFERENCES

Amichai-Hamburger, Y., & McKenna, K. Y. A. (2006). The contact hypothesis reconsidered: Interacting via the Internet. *Journal of Computer-Mediated Communication*, *11*, 825–843, doi: 10.1111/j.1083-6101.2006.00037.x.

Arseneault, L., Walsh, E., Trzesniewskizf, K., Newcombe, R., Caspi, A., & Moffitt, T. E. (2006). Bullying victimization uniquely contributes to adjustment problems in young children: A nationally representative cohort study. *Pediatrics*, *118*, 130–138.

Bacchini, D., Esposito, G., & Affuso, G. (2009). *Social Experience and School Bullying*, *32*, 17–32, doi: 10.1002/casp.

Baldry, A. C. (1998). Bullying among Italian middle school students: Combining methods to understand aggressive behaviours and victimisation. *School Psychology International*, *19*, 155–168.

Besag, V. (1989). *Bullies and victims in schools*. Milton Keynes, UK: Open University Press.

Bhat, C. S. (2008). Cyber bullying: Overview and strategies for school counsellors, guidance officers, and all school personnel. *Australian Journal of Guidance and Counselling*, *18*, 53–66, doi: 10.1375/ajgc.18.1.53.

Bjorkqvist, K. (1994). Sex differences in physical, verbal, and indirect aggression: A review of recent research. *Sex Roles*, *30*, 177–188.

Bjorkqvist, K. (2001). Comments to "Top ten challenges for understanding gender and aggression in children: Why can't we all just get along?": Different names, same issues. *Social Development*, *10*, 272–274.

Björkqvist, K., Lagerspetz, K., & Kaukiainen, A. (1992). Do girls manipulate and boys fight? Developmental trends in regard to direct and indirect aggression. *Aggressive Behavior*, *18*, 117–127.

Blair, J. (2003). New breed of bullies torment their peers on the Internet. *Education Week*, *22*, 6–7.

Boivin, M., Hymel, S., & Burkowski, W. M. (1995). The roles of social withdrawal, peer rejection, and victimization by peers in predicting loneliness and depressed mood in childhood. *Development and Psychopathology*, *7*, 765–785, doi: 10.1017/s0954579400006830.

Bollmer, J. M., Milich, R., Harris, M. J., & Maras, M. A. (2005). A friend in need: The role of friendship quality as protective factor in peer victimization and bullying. *Journal of Interpersonal Violence*, *20*, 701–712.

Bosworth, K., Espelage, D. L., & Simon, T. R. (1999). Factors associated with bullying behavior in middle school students. *The Journal of Early Adolescence*, *19*, 341–362, doi: 10.1177/0272431699019003003.

Butler, D., Kift, S., & Campbell, M. A. (2010). Cyber bullying in schools and the law: Is there an effective means of addressing the power imbalance? *eLaw Journal: Murdoch University Electronic Journal of Law*, *16*, 84.

Calvete, E., Orue, I., Estévez, A., Villardón, L., & Padilla, P. (2010). Cyberbullying in adolescents: Modalities and aggressors' profile. *Computers in Human Behavior*, *26*, 1128–1135.

Campbell, M. A. (2005). Cyber bullying: An old problem in a new guise? *Australian Journal of Guidance and Counselling*, *15*, 68–76.

Canning, V. (2010). Who's human? Developing sociological understandings of the rights of women raped in conflict. *The International Journal of Human Rights*, *14*, 849–864.

Caravita, S. C. S., Pöyhönen, V., Rajala, I., & Salmivalli, C. (2011). The architecture of high status among Finnish youth. *British Journal of Developmental Psychology*, *29*, 668–679, doi: 10.1111/j.2044-835X.2011.02034.x.

Coyne, S. M., Archer, J., & Eslea, M. (2006). "We're not friends anymore! Unless...": The frequency and harmfulness of indirect, relational, and social aggression. *Aggressive Behavior*, *32*, 294–307.

Craig, W. M. (1998). The relationship among bullying, victimization, depression, anxiety, and aggression in elementary school children. *Personality and Individual Differences*, *24*, 123–130, doi: 10.1016/S0191-8869(97)00145-1.

Crapanzano, A. M., Frick, P. J., & Terranova, A. M. (2010). Patterns of physical and relational aggression in a school-based sample of boys and girls. *Journal of Abnormal Child Psychology*, *38*, 433–445, doi:10.1007/s10802-009-9376-3.

Crick, N. R. (1995). Relational aggression: The role of intent attributions, feelings of distress, and provocation type. *Development and Psychopathology*, *7*, 313–322.

Crick, N. R., Casas, J. F., & Mosher., M. (1997). Relational and overt aggression in preschool. *Developmental Psychology*, *33*, 579–588.

Crick, N. R., & Dodge, K. A. (1996). Social information-processing mechanisms in reactive and proactive aggression. *Child Development*, *67*, 993–1002, doi: 10.1111/j.1467-8624.1996.tb01778.x.

Crick, N. R., & Grotpeter, J. K. (1995). Relational aggression, gender, and social-psychological adjustment. *Child Development*, *66*, 710–722.

Dehue, F., Bolman, C., & Vollink, T. (2008). Cyberbullying: Youngsters' experiences and parental perception. *Cyberpsychology & Behavior: The Impact of the Internet, Multimedia and Virtual Reality on Behavior and Society*, *11*, 217–223.

Diamanduros, T., Downs, E., & Jenkins, S. J. (2008). The role of school psychologists in the assessment, prevention, and intervention of cyberbullying. *Psychology in the Schools*, *45*, 693–704, doi: 10.1002/pits.20335.

Dodge, K. A., & Coie, J. D. (1987). Social-information-processing factors in reactive and proactive aggression in children's peer groups. *Journal of Personality and Social Psychology*, *53*, 1146–1158.

Dooley, J., Pyzalski, J., & Cross, D. (2009). Cyberbullying versus face-to-face bullying. *A theoretical and conceptual review. Zeitschrift fur Psychologie/Journal of Psychology*, *217*, 182–188.

Epley, N., & Kruger, J. (2005). When what you type isn't what they read: The perseverance of stereotypes and expectancies over e-mail. *Journal of Experimental Social Psychology*, *41*, 414–422.

Erdur-Baker, Ö. (2010). Cyberbullying and its correlation to traditional bullying, gender and frequent and risky usage of internet-mediated communication tools. *New Media & Society*, *12*, 109–125, doi: 10.1177/1461444809341260.

Essau, C. A., Sasagawa, S., & Frick, P. J. (2006). Psychometric properties of the Alabama Parenting Questionnaire. *Journal of Child and Family Studies*, *15*, 597–616, doi: 10.1007/s10826-006-9036-y.

Forero, R., McLellan, L., Rissel, C., & Baum, A. (1999). Bullying behaviour and psychosocial health among school students in New South Wales, Australia. *British Medical Journal*, *319*, 344–348.

Galen, B. R., & Underwood, M. K. (1997). A developmental investigation of social aggression among children. *Developmental Psychology*, *33*, 589–600.

Garandeau, C. F., & Cillessen, A. H. N. (2006). From indirect aggression to invisible aggression: A conceptual view on bullying and peer group manipulation. *Aggression and Violent Behavior*, *11*, 612–625, doi: 10.1016/j.avb.2005.08.005.

Gini, G. (2008). Associations between bullying behaviour, psychosomatic complaints, emotional and behavioural problems. *Journal of Paediatrics and Child Health*, *44*, 492–497, doi: 10.1111/j.1440-1754.2007.01155.x.

Goldbaum, S., Craig, W. M., Pepler, D., & Connolly, J. (2003). Developmental trajectories of victimization: Identifying risk and protective factors. *Journal of Applied School Psychology*, *19*, 139–156.

Guadagno, R. E., & Cialdini, R. B. (2002). Online persuasion: An examination of gender differences in computer-mediated interpersonal influence. *Group Dynamics: Theory Research and Practice*, *6*, 38–51, doi: 10.1037//1089-2699.6.1.38.

Hartman, R., & Stage, S. A. (2000). The relationship between social information processing and in-school suspension for students with behavioral disorders. *Behavioral Disorders*, *25*, 183–195.

Hinduja, S., & Patchin, J. W. (2008). Cyberbullying: An exploratory analysis of factors related to offending and victimization. *Deviant Behavior*, *29*, 129–156.

Katz, D., Allport, F. H., & Jenness, M. B. (1931). *Students' attitudes; a report of the Syracuse University reaction study*. Oxford, UK: Craftsman Press.

Kerawalla, L., & Crook, C. (2002). Children's computer use at home and school: Context and continuity. *British Educational Research Journal*, *22*, 751–771.

Kift, S., Campbell, M. A., & Butler, D. (2010). Cyberbullying in social networking sites and blogs: Legal issues for young people and schools. *Journal of Law, Information and Science*, *20*, 60–97.

Kimborough, A. M., Guadagno, R. E., Muscanell, N. L., & Dill, J. (2012). *Gender differences in technology use: Women connect more than do men*. Manuscript submitted for publication.

Kowalski, R., Limber, S., & Agatston, P. W. (2008). *Cyber bullying*. Malden, MA: Blackwell Publishing.

Latane, B., & Darley, J. M. (1968). Group inhibition of bystander intervention in emergencies. *Journal of Personality and Social Psychology*, *10*, 215–221, doi: 10.1037/h0026570.

Law, D. M., Shapka, J. D., Domene, J. F., & Gagné, M. H. (2012). Are cyberbullies really bullies? An investigation of reactive and proactive online aggression. *Computers in Human Behavior*, *28*, 664–672, doi: 10.1016/j.chb.2011.11.013.

Law, D. M., Shapka, J. D., & Olson, B. F. (2010). To control or not to control? Parenting behaviors and adolescent online aggression. *Computers in Human Behavior*, *26*, 1651–1656.

Li, Q. (2006). Cyberbullying in schools: A research of gender differences. *School Psychology International*, *27*, 157–170, doi: 10.1177/0143034306064547.

Li, Q. (2007). New bottle but old wine: A research of cyberbullying in schools. *Computers in Human Behavior*, *23*, 1777–1791, doi: 10.1016/j.chb.2005.10.005.

Li, Q. (2008). A cross-cultural comparison of adolescents' experience related to cyberbullying. *Educational Research*, *50*, 223–234, doi: 10.1080/00131880802309333.

Lochman, J. E., & Wells, K. C. (2002). Contextual social-cognitive mediators and child outcome: A test of the theoretical model in the Coping Power program. *Development and Psychopathology*, *14*, 945–967, doi: doi:10.1017/S0954579402004157.

McKenna, K. Y. A., & Bargh, J. A. (2000). Plan 9 from cyberspace: The implications of the Internet for personality and social psychology. *Personality and Social Psychology Review*, *4*, 57–75, doi: 10.1207/s15327957pspr0401_6.

Menesini, E., & Nocentini, A. (2009). Cyberbullying definition and measurement. *Zeitschrift für Psychologi /Journal of Psychology*, *217*, 230–232, doi: 10.1027/0044-3409.217.4.230.

Menesini, E., Nocentini, A., Palladino, B. E., Frisén, A., Berne, S., Ortega-Ruiz, R., Calmaestra, J., Scheithauer, H., Schultze-Krumbholz, A., Luik, P., Naruskov, K., Blaya, C., Berthaud, J., & Smith, P. K. (2012). *Cyberpsychology, Behavior, and Social Networking*, *15*, 455–463.

Menesini, E., & Spiel, C. (2012). Introduction: Cyberbullying: Development, consequences, risk and protective factors. *European Journal of Developmental Psychology*, *9*, 163–167.

Mishna, F. (2004). A qualitative study of bullying from multiple perspectives. *Children & Schools*, *26*, 234–247.

Mishna, F., Wiener, J., & Pepler, D. (2008). Some of my best friends: Experiences of bullying within friendships. *School Psychology International*, *29*, 549–573.

Morton, F. S., Zettelmeyer, F., & Silva-Risso, J. (2003). Consumer information and discrimination: Does the Internet affect the pricing of new cars to women and minorities? *Quantitative Marketing and Economics*, *1*, 65–92.

Nansel, T. R., Overpeck, M., Pilla, R. S., Ruan, W. J., Simons Morton, B., & Scheidt, P. (2001). Bullying behaviors among US youth: Prevalence and association with psychological adjustment. *Journal of the American Medical Association*, *285*, 2094–2100.

Noble, T. (2003). Nobody left to hate. *EQ Australia*, *4*, 8–9.

Olweus, D. (1991). Bully/victim problems among school children: Basic facts and effects of a school based intervention program. In D. Pepler & K. Rubin (Eds.), *The development and treatment of childhood aggression* (pp. 411–446). Hillsdale, NJ: Lawrence Erlbaum Associates Inc.

Olweus, D. (1994). Bullying at school: Basic facts and effects of a school based intervention program. *Journal of Child Psychology and Psychiatry*, *35*, 1171–1190, doi: 10.1111/j.1469-7610.1994.tb01229.x.

Orobio de Castro, B., Veerman, J. W., Koops, W., Bosch, J. D., & Monshouwer, H. J. (2002). Hostile attribution of intent and aggressive behavior: A meta-analysis. *Child Development*, *73*, 916–934.

Owens, L., Shute, R., & Slee, P. (2007). "They do it just to show off." Year 9 girls', boys' and their teachers' explanations for boys' aggression to girls. *International Journal of Adolescence and Youth*, *13*, 343–360.

Patchin, J. W., & Hinduja, S. (2006). Bullies move beyond the schoolyard: A preliminary look at cyberbullying. *Youth Violence and Juvenile Justice*, *4*, 148–169, doi: 10.1177/1541204006286288.

Pellegrini, A. D., & Bartini, M. (2001). Dominance in early adolescent boys: Affiliative and aggressive dimensions and possible functions. *Merrill-Palmer Quarterly*, *47*, 142–163, doi: 10.1353/mpq.2001.0004.

Peter, J., Valkenburg, P. M., & Schouten, A. P. (2005). Developing a model of adolescent friendship formation on the Internet. *CyberPsychology and Behavior*, *8*, 423–430.

Piazza, J., & Bering, J. M. (2009). Evolutionary cyber-psychology: Applying arevolutionary framework to internet behavior. *Computers in Human Behavior, 25*, 1258–1269.

Postmes, T., Spears, R., & Lea, M. (2002). Intergroup differentiation in computer mediated communication: Effects of depersonalization. *Group Dynamics, 6*, 3–15.

Pozzoli, T., & Gini, G. (2012). Why do bystanders of bullying help or not? A multidimensional model. *The Journal of Early Adolescence*. doi: 10.1177/0272431612440172.

Renati, R., Berrone, C., & Zanetti, M.A. (2012). Morally disengaged and unempathic: Do cyberbullies fit these definitions? An exploratory study. *Cyberpsychology, Behavior, and Social Networking, 15*, 391–398, doi:10.1089/cyber.2012.0046.

Ridout, V., Roberts, D. F., & Foehr, U. G. (2005). *Generation M: Media in the lives of 8–18 year-olds: Executive summary*. Menlo Park, CA: Henry J. Kaiser Family Foundation.

Rivers, I., & Smith, P. K. (1994). Types of bullying behaviour and their correlates. *Aggressive Behavior, 20*, 359–368, doi: 10.1002/1098-2337(1994)20:5<359::aid-ab2480200503>3.0.co;2-j.

Roland, E., & Idsøe, T. (2001). Aggression and bullying. *Aggressive Behavior, 27*, 446–462.

Salmivalli, C., & Nieminen, E. (2002). Proactive and reactive aggression among school bullies, victims, and bully-victims. *Aggressive Behavior, 28*, 30–44. doi: 10.1002/ab.90004.

Salmivalli, C., & Voeten, M. (2004). Connections between attitudes, group norms, and behaviour in bullying situations. *International Journal of Behavioral Development, 28*, 246–258, doi: 10.1080/01650250344000488.

Salmivalli, C., Voeten, M., & Poskiparta, E. (2011). Bystanders matter: Associations between reinforcing, defending, and the frequency of bullying behavior in classrooms. *Journal of Clinical Child & Adolescent Psychology, 40*, 668–676, doi: 10.1080/15374416.2011.597090.

Schenk, A. M., & Fremouw, W. J. (2012). Prevalence, psychological impact, and coping of cyberbully victims among college students. *Journal of School Violence, 11*, 21–37, doi: 10.1080/15388220.2011.630310.

Schwartz, D., Dodge, K. A., Coie, J. D., Hubbard, J. A., Cillessen, A. H. N., Lemerise, E. A., & Bateman, H. (1998). Socialcognitive and behavioral correlates of aggression and victimization in boys' play groups. *Journal of Abnormal Child Psychology, 26*, 431–440.

Shariff, S. (2009). *Confronting cyber-bullying: What schools need to know to control misconduct and avoid legal consequences*. New York: Cambridge University Press.

Shelton, K. K., Frick, P. J., & Wootton, J. (1996). Assessment of parenting practices in families of elementary school-age children. *Journal of Clinical Child Psychology, 25*, 317–329.

Slonje, R., & Smith, P. K. (2008). Cyberbullying: Another main type of bullying? *Scandinavian Journal of Psychology, 49*, 147–154.

Smith, P. K., & Boulton, M. (1990). Rough-and-tumble play, aggression and dominance: Perception and behaviour in children's encounters. *Human Development*, *33*, 271–282.

Smith, P. K., Mahdavi, J., Carvalho, M., Fisher, S., Russell, S., & Tippet, N. (2008). Cyberbullying: Its nature and impact in secondary school pupils. *Journal of Child Psychology and Psychiatry*, *49*, 376–385.

Smith, P. K., Mahdavi, J., Carvalho, M., & Tippett, N. (2006). An investigation into cyberbullying, its forms, awareness and impact and the relationship between age and gender in cyberbullying Research Brief No. RBX03-06. In P. K. Smith & S. Sharp (Eds.), *School bullying: Insights and perspectives*. London: DfES, Routledge.

Smith, P. K., & Shu, S. (2000). What good schools can do about bullying: Findings from a survey in English schools after a decade of research and action. *Childhood*, *7*, 193–212.

Solberg, M. E., & Olweus, D. (2003). Prevalence estimation of school bullying with the Olweus Bully/Victim Questionnaire. *Aggressive Behavior*, *29*, 239–268, doi: 10.1002/ab.10047.

Sourander, A., Helstela, L., Helenius, H., & Piha, J. (2000). Persistence of bullying from childhood to adolescence: A longitudinal 8-year follow-up study. *Child Abuse and Neglect*, *24*, 873–881.

Stattin, H., & Kerr, M. (2000). Parental Monitoring: A reinterpretation. *Child Development*, *71*, 1072–1085.

Stauffer, S., Heath, M. A., Coyne, S. M., & Ferrin, S. (2012). High school teachers' perceptions of cyberbullying prevention and intervention strategies. *Psychology in the Schools*, *49*, 352–367, doi: 10.1002/pits.21603.

Tani, F., Greenman, P. S., Schneider, B. H., & Fregoso, M. (2003). Bullying and the Big Five. *School Psychology International*, *24*, 131–146, doi: 10.1177/0143034303024002001.

Teräsahjo, T., & Salmivalli, C. (2003). "She is not actually bullied." The discourse of harassment in student groups. *Aggressive Behavior*, *29*, 134–154, doi: 10.1002/ab.10045.

Tokunaga, R. S. (2010). Following you home from school: A critical review and synthesis of research on cyberbullying victimization. *Computers in Human Behavior*, *26*, 277–287, doi: 10.1016/j.chb.2009.11.014.

Underwood, M. K., Galen, B. R., & Paquette, J. A. (2001). Top ten challenges for understanding gender and aggression in children: Why can't we all just get along? *Social Development*, *10*, 248–266, doi: 10.1111/1467-9507.00162.

Unnever, J. D. (2005). Bullies, aggressive victims, and victims: Are they distinct groups? *Aggressive Behavior*, *31*, 153–171, doi: 10.1002/ab.20083.

Walrave, M., & Heirman, W. (2011). Cyberbullying: Predicting victimisation and perpetration. *Children & Society*, *25*, 59–72.

Wang, J., Iannotti, R. J., & Nansel, T. R. (2009). School bullying among adolescents in the United States: Physical, verbal, relational, and cyber. *Journal of Adolescent Health*, *45*, 368–375, doi: 10.1016/j.jadohealth.2009.03.021.

Ward, C. C., & Tracy, T. J. G. (2004). Relation of shyness with aspects of online relationship involvement. *Journal of Social and Personal Relationships*, *21*, 611–623.

Willard, N. (2007). The authority and responsibility of school officials in responding to cyberbullying. *Journal of Adolescent Health*, *41*, 64–65.

Ybarra, M. L., & Mitchell, K. J. (2004a). Youth engaging in online harassment: With caregiver–child relationships, Internet use, and personal characteristics. *Journal of Adolescence*, *27*, 319–336.

Ybarra, M. L., & Mitchell, K. J. (2004b). Online aggressor/targets, aggressors, and targets: A comparison of associated youth characteristics. *Journal of Child Psychology and Psychiatry*, *45*, 1308–1316.

Developmental trajectories of adolescent victimization: Predictors and outcomes

Leanne Lester[1], Donna Cross[1], Julian Dooley[2], and Thérèse Shaw[1]
[1]Child Health Promotion Research Centre, Edith Cowan University, Mt Lawley, WA, Australia
[2]Sellenger Centre for Research in Law, Justice and Social Change, Edith Cowan University, Mt Lawley, WA, Australia

Chronic victimization negatively affects mental health, making it crucial to understand the key predictive social health (e.g., loneliness, isolation) factors. Evidence suggests that the effects of victimization are worse over the transition from primary to secondary school. Longitudinal data from 1810 students transitioning were used to identify victimization trajectory groups, classified as low increasing, low stable, medium stable, and not bullied. Adolescents with poorer social health were more likely to be in the increasing and stable victimized group than in the not bullied group. Students in the low increasing victimized group had poorer mental health outcomes than those in the stable and not bullied groups. The results of this study have important implications for the type and timing of school-based interventions aimed at reducing victimization and the harms caused by long-term exposure.

School bullying, defined as a type of repeated aggressive behavior involving the systematic abuse of power through unjustified acts intended to inflict harm (Smith, 2004), has a traumatic impact on all involved regardless of role

We thank Stacey Waters and Melanie Epstein for their contributions to the Supportive Schools Project (SSP) project, and the SSP study schools and their staff, parents, and students. The SSP Project and this study were funded by the Western Australian Health Promotion Foundation (Healthway) and the research supported by the Child Health Promotion Research Centre (CHPRC) at Edith Cowan University, Western Australia.
This research was funded through a Healthway Scholarship.

(perpetrators, victims, bully-victims, or bystanders), with the level of trauma related to frequency of exposure (Carney, 2008). Exposure to chronic victimization can lead to traumatic reactions which may result in greater expressed physical, psychological. and emotional symptoms (Garbarino, 2001), which in turn may contribute to lasting long-term effects (Carney, 2008). Stress from physical and verbal bullying has been found to elevate the levels of cortisol and may impact adolescent long-term mental health and memory functioning, affecting school achievement (Vaillancourt et al., 2011). Many students who are chronically victimized throughout school are maladjusted (Rosen et al., 2009), suffer stress later in life (Newman, Holden, & Delville, 2005), and are bullied as adults (Smith, Singer, Hoel, & Cooper, 2003). Genetic differences may result in some frequently bullied children being more vulnerable to the emotional effects of bullying victimization than others (Sugden et al., 2010). Bond, Carlin, Thomas, Rubin, and Patton (2001) reported that victimization rates were generally high (approximately 50%) and stable with two-thirds of adolescents who were frequently victimized 1 year later. A more recent Australian study found approximately one-quarter of adolescents are victimized every few weeks or more often (Cross et al., 2009).

Given the high prevalence of chronic adolescent victimization and the associated consequences, it is important to understand the developmental pathways of victimization. In adolescence victimization decreases from a high following the transition from primary to secondary school to lower levels at the end of secondary school with the development of social understanding, shifting norms against specific types of victimization (Nansel et al., 2001), and the priority of popularity (LaFontana & Cillessen, 2010) in the peer group. The use of victimization trajectories allows the longitudinal examination of victimization, revealing those who are chronically victimized as well as associated predictors and outcomes of victimization trajectories. Previous longitudinal studies, focused on primary school (children Grade 3 through to Grade 7) victimization trajectory analyses (Boivin, Petitclerc, Feng, & Barker, 2010; Goldbaum, Craig, Pepler, & Connolly, 2003), found approximately 80% of students followed a low or non-victim trajectory, with the remainder of victims following stable, increasing, or decreasing victimization trajectories over time. Data in these studies were collected over a 4-year and 3-year time period respectively. Gender differences in the number and shape of victimization trajectories are expected due to the type of victimization experienced by males and females (males are more likely to experience physical victimization; females covert relational victimization; Pepler, Jiang, Craig, & Connolly, 2008) and the higher prevalence of victimization reported by males over females during the transition from primary to secondary school (Cross et al., 2009).

This study examined developmental victimization trajectories of students from the end of primary school (Grade 7 – age 12) to the end of the second year of secondary school (Grade 9 – age 14). Among Australian students, an increase in bullying behavior appears to occur around age 11 and immediately following the transition from primary school to secondary school (Cross et al., 2009). This increase in bullying behaviors may be due to a combination of factors including greater academic competition, teachers' poorer attitudes towards bullying, a reduced sense of a positive school ethos in secondary schools relative to primary schools, and a peak in social aggression (Pellegrini, 2002; Pellegrini & Bartini, 2000; Underwood, Beron, & Rosen, 2009). Adolescence coincides with the transition from primary to secondary school contributing to a major change in social structure, with students often needing to develop new friendships and define their place in a new social hierarchy (Pellegrini & Bartini, 2000).

It has been demonstrated that victimized students possess ineffective coping skills in both information processing and social behavior domains (Smith, Talamelli, Cowie, Naylor, & Chauhan, 2004). Poor coping skills have been found to lead to increased stress levels, which have an impact on mental health (Aldwin, 2011). Consistently, the stress-coping model, which proposes that victimized students are more likely to exhibit psychological distress if they feel unsupported, can illuminate the mental health impact of victimization (Cassidy & Taylor, 2005). Social health (i.e., the ability to get along with others, dealing with social institutions and societal mores) is associated with a greater capacity to cope with social problems (e.g., bullying). Importantly, being socially healthy can be protective against victimization over the transition period. Consistently, Lester, Cross, Dooley, and Shaw (2012a) found significant reciprocal causal pathways between social health factors and victimization over the transition period, with students feeling a greater connectedness to school, feeling more safe at school and having greater peer support reporting less victimization. Alternatively, students feeling less connectedness to school, feeling less safe at school, feeling more lonely, and having less peer support reported greater victimization. This study focused on the Grade 7 social health factors (i.e., feeling less lonely at school, connectedness to school, peer support, and feeling safe at school) that predict membership to victimization trajectory groups. This study focused on the Grade 7 social health factors (i.e., loneliness at school, connectedness to school, peer support, and feeling safe at school) that predict membership to victimization trajectory groups. Importantly, the social health factors investigated in this study are all amenable to school intervention (Libbey, 2004; Menesini, Codecasa, Benelli, & Cowie, 2003; Naylor & Cowie, 1999).

Researchers have found bullying victimization to be longitudinally associated with depression (Bond et al., 2001; Hawker & Boulton, 2000;

Kaltiala-Heino, Rimpela, Rantanen, & Rimpela, 2000; Lester, Cross, Dooley, & Shaw, 2012b; O'Brennan, Bradshaw, & Sawyer, 2009; Roland, 2002; Sweeting, Young, West, & Der, 2006; Ybarra, 2004), anxiety (Kaltiala-Heino et al., 2000; Lester, Cross, Dooley, & Shaw, 2012b; Salmon, James, & Smith, 1998), psychosomatic complaints (Fekkes, Pijpers, & Verloove-Vanhorick, 2004; Kaltiala-Heino et al., 2000) and suicidal ideation (Kaltiala-Heino, Rimpela, Marttunen, Rimpela, & Rantanen, 1999; Rigby & Slee, 1999; Salmon, James, Cassidy, & Javaloyes, 2000). Persistent victimization is a strong predictor of the onset of depression and anxiety (Bond et al., 2001) with those chronically victimized showing more negative effects (Menesini, 2009) than those only recently victimized. In this study the mental health outcomes of adolescents in the different victimization trajectory groups will be compared.

Hence this paper aims to use longitudinal data to model the developmental trajectories of victimization during and following the transition from primary to secondary school and to determine the existence of gender differences in the shape and number of trajectory paths. The social health predictors of trajectory group membership will also be explored, with poorer social health at the end of primary school (Grade 7) expected to be associated with chronic victimization group membership. Those in chronic victimization trajectories are also expected to have poorer mental health outcomes in secondary school (Grade 9) than those in low or non-victim trajectories.

METHOD

The data in this study were taken from a larger longitudinal study, the Supportive Schools Project (SSP) conducted in Perth, Western Australia, which aimed to enhance the capacity of secondary schools to implement a whole-of-school bullying reduction intervention. Data from only the study comparison schools have been used, as the intervention is not a focus of this paper. The study was approved by the Edith Cowan University Human Research Ethics Committee and the relevant school authorities.

Sampling and data collection

To reduce the rate of transition attrition as students move from primary to secondary schools, secondary schools affiliated with the Catholic Education Office (CEO) of Western Australia were recruited to participate in the study. Students within Australian Catholic schools are more likely than students attending schools in other sectors (e.g., government schools) to move from primary to secondary schools in intact groups. Cohort data were collected during the Supportive Schools Project (SSP) from 3462 students from 21 of the 28 Catholic secondary schools in Western Australia. The seven schools that declined to participate cited other priorities within their school and demanding staff workloads. All CEO schools were stratified according to the total number of students enrolled at the school and each school's socio-economic status (SES) and were randomly selected and randomly assigned to an intervention or comparison group (Cross, Hall, Waters, & Hamilton, 2008).

Data used in this paper were collected from students assigned to comparison schools in four waves from 2005 to 2007. To collect data relating to pre-transition experience, all Grade 7 students enrolled to commence in Grade 8 at each of the 21 participating secondary schools received a baseline survey while in Grade 7 at their respective primary schools. Parents of Grade 8 students at the 21 secondary schools, who had not been recruited in Grade 7 as they were not on the school enrolment lists, were approached for consent for their child's participation at the first follow-up.

The student cohort was surveyed at the end of Grade 7 (mean age 12 years), the beginning and end of Grade 8 (mean age 13 years old), and the end of Grade 9 (mean age 14 years old). In total 3462 (92% of the total recruited) students completed questionnaires at least at one time point, with 3123 (90%) responding to at least three of the four data collection points. One half of the students surveyed were male and 70% attended a co-educational secondary school versus a single sex secondary school. Responses from only the students from the SSP study comparison schools were used in the analysis detailed below.

All schools involved in the study had specific written bullying policies. School administrators, pastoral care staff, and some teachers typically contributed to the development and writing of their school's bullying prevention and management component of the school's behavior management plan. The bullying prevention and management policies typically covered a definition of bullying, the school's position and response in relation to bullying, the management of bullying incidents, and rights and responsibilities of the whole school community.

Active consent (where parents gave written permission for their child to participate) was requested from all parents; if any parents did not respond to this active consent approach up to two follow-up letters were sent to parents requesting their passive consent where they were required to opt-out if they did not wish their child to participate (Ellickson & Hawes, 1989). This two layered consent process resulted in 93% of parents whose children were enrolled in the 21 recruited secondary schools consenting to their child participating in the study.

Measures

Victimization

To assess physical, relational, and verbal victimization, a seven-item categorical index adapted from items/scales developed by Rigby and Slee (1998) and Olweus (1996) was used. The items assessed physical (hit, kicked, and pushed around; had money or other things broken or taken away from them; made to feel afraid they would get hurt), verbal (made fun of and teased in a hurtful way; called mean and hurtful names), and relational (students ignored them, didn't let them join in, or left them out on purpose; students told lies about them and tried to make other students not like them) bullying during the current term (10 weeks) at school. Students were asked how often they were bullied and rated each item on a 5-point scale (1 = ever, 2 = once or twice, 3 = every few weeks, 4 = about once a week, 5 = most days). A definition of bullying, supported by illustrations of the behaviors, was provided in the questionnaire. Confirmatory factor analysis performed on the victimization scale confirmed its unidimensionality (CFI > 0.9, SMR < 0.10 at all time points). A victimization score was calculated at each time point for each student by averaging the seven items with a higher score reflecting more experiences of victimization (average alpha = 0.86).

Peer support

The peer support at school scale (adapted from the 24-item Perceptions of Peer Social Support Scale (Ladd, Kochenderfer, & Coleman, 1996); comprised 11 items (How often would students: choose you on their team; tell you you're good at things; explain something if you didn't understand; invite you to do things with them; help you if you are hurt; miss you if you weren't at school; help you if something is bothering you; ask to work with you; help you if other students treat you badly; ask you to join in when alone; and share things with you?) measured on a 3-point scale (1 = never, 2 = sometimes, 3 = lots of times). A factor analysis performed on the adapted peer support scale confirmed its unidimensionality (CFI > 0.9, SMR < 0.10 at all time points). A peer support score at each time point was calculated for each student by averaging all items, higher scores reflecting greater feelings of peer support (average alpha = 0.88).

Loneliness

Loneliness was measured using seven items adapted from Cassidy and Asher's 15-item loneliness at school scale (J. Cassidy & Asher, 1992). The seven items (I feel alone at school; I have lots of friends to talk to at school; It's hard for me to make friends at school; I have nobody to talk to in my classes; I don't have anyone to spend time with at school; I'm lonely at school; I feel left out of things at school) were measured on a 5-point scale ranging from strongly disagree to strongly agree. Confirmatory factor analysis confirmed the unidimensionality of the scale (CFI > 0.9, SMR < 0.10 at all time points). A mean loneliness score was calculated at each time point for each student, with higher scores reflected greater feelings of loneliness (average alpha $= 0.72$).

Connectedness

The connectedness to school scale comprised four items adapted from the Resnick et al. (1997) six-item School Connectedness Scale (I feel close to people at school; I feel like I am part of this school; I am happy to be at school; the teachers treat students fairly) measured on a 5-point scale (1 = unsure, 2 = never, 3 = sometimes, 4 = usually, 5 = always). Unidimensionality was confirmed through factor analysis (CFI > 0.9, SMR < 0.10 at all time points). For each student at each time point an average school connectedness score was calculated, with a higher score reflecting greater feelings of connectedness (average alpha $= 0.80$).

Safety

Safety at school was a single item adapted from Rigby and Slee's Peer Relations Questionnaire (1998) and measured on a 3-point scale (1 = No, I never feel safe at school, 2 = Yes, some of the time, 3 = Yes, all or most of the time) for each time point, with a higher value reflecting greater feelings of safety at school.

Mental health

Self-reported depression and anxiety were assessed using the Depression Anxiety Stress Scale (Lovibond & Lovibond, 1995) which comprised seven items relating to depression and seven items related to anxiety measured on a 4-point scale (ranging from 0 = not at all to 3 = applied to me very much, or most of the time). A depression score and an anxiety score were calculated at each time point for each student by adding the items, with higher scores reflecting greater feelings of depression (average alpha $= 0.89$) and anxiety (average alpha $= 0.82$).

Data collection

Students completed the baseline questionnaires in Term 4 of the final year of primary school (Grade 7, average age 11 years) and then follow-up questionnaires again at the beginning and then the end of the first year after transition to secondary school (Grade 8, average age 12 years) and about 12 months later (i.e., at the end of Grade 9).

Due to the movement of students between schools, baseline student data were collected differently from follow-up student data. At baseline parents were sent a copy of the student questionnaire with the consent form, and a reply paid envelope to return the consent form and if they agreed, their child's completed questionnaire. Parents who did not respond were sent up to two follow-up letters. Follow-up data collections in Grades 8 and 9 were conducted by trained research staff who administered questionnaires to students during class time using a standardized protocol. Students who did not have consent to participate in the study completed alternate learning activities.

Statistical analysis

Analyses were conducted using MPlus v6 and STATA v12. Victimization trajectories were modeled on the comparison group within MPlus with the censored normal distribution used to account for the censoring at the lower bounds of the victimization scale. A polynomial relationship was used to link victimization with time. All four time points from longitudinal data collected at the end of Grade 7 to the end of Grade 9 were used in the calculation of trajectories. Missing data at each time point were handled through Full Information Maximum Likelihood (FIML) estimation in Mplus v6 enabling the use of all students with at least one valid score in the analyses. FIML assumes missing at random and produces unbiased parameter estimates and standard errors of the data (Wothke, 1998). Separate multinomial logistic regression models (using robust standard error estimation to account for school level clustering in the data) were fitted in Stata v12 for males and females and were used to determine whether the social health predictors of loneliness, connectedness to school, safety at school, and peer support at the end of primary school (Grade 7) could individually be used to predict the identified victimization trajectory groups. Models were run using different trajectory groups as the reference group to explore differences in the likelihood of group memberships. Separate random effect Tobit regression models, taking into account the highly skewed and clustered nature of the data were fitted in Stata v12 to determine differences in students' mental health outcomes (Grade 9) for the different victimization trajectory groups. Mental health measured at the end of primary school (Grade 7) was controlled for in the Tobit regression analyses.

RESULTS

Trajectories of victimization

Developmental trajectories of victimization were identified using the semi-parametric group-based trajectory approach (Nagin, 2005). The dependent variable was victimization measured at the four time points for comparison group students only. This paper uses a continuous victimization measure for each student with a higher score reflecting greater victimization.

To determine the best-fitting models, models were compared through an examination of fit statistics as well as theoretical justification and interpretability. Fit statistics examined included the Bayesian Information Criterion (BIC; a smaller BIC value represents a better fit), the Lo-Mendell-Rubin Likelihood Ratio Test (LMR; comparing the current model against the model with one less group should give a LMR and BLRT p-value less than 0.05; Jung & Wickrama, 2008; Nylund, Asparouhov, & Muthén, 2007). To ensure optimal solutions were obtained from the analysis rather than local maxima, 500 random sets of starting values were used in the model. Application of the minimum BIC for model selection did not result in the determination of a clear best model with BIC improving with the addition of groups. The LMR-BLRT test of model fit indicated that increasing the model from four classes to five classes was not significant ($p = .14$). Given this non-significant result and the small proportion of students in the fifth high stable class, the four-class model was chosen as optimal.

Figure 1 shows the distinct trajectories of the four-group model for victimization. The largest group (52% of the sample) was the *low stable* group. This group comprised students who reported low levels of victimization across the four time points. The *not bullied* group (40%) comprised students who did not report victimization over the time period. The *low increasing* victimization group (4%) comprised students who reported low levels of victimization at the end of primary school and the beginning of secondary school, with victimization increasing to high levels by the end of the second year of secondary school. The *medium stable* group (4%) was made up of students who reported medium levels of victimization at the end of primary school and during the first two years of secondary school. An examination of the different types of victimization (physical, verbal, and relational) showed higher levels of verbal and relational victimization than physical victimization in all trajectory groups at all time points for both males and females (Table 1). No significant differences between the levels of each type of victimization between each victimization trajectory were found for females, however males in the lower increasing trajectory group had significantly lower physical victimization than other trajectory groups at the end of Grade 8.

Students were assigned to a trajectory group based on their individual probability scores. The distributions indicated that trajectory groups differed significantly on the proportion of male and female students ($\chi^2 = 48.9$, $p < .001$) with distributions within the *not bullied* group higher for females (45%) than males (36%), whereas the distributions within the *low increasing* and *medium stable* groups were higher for males (6.2% and

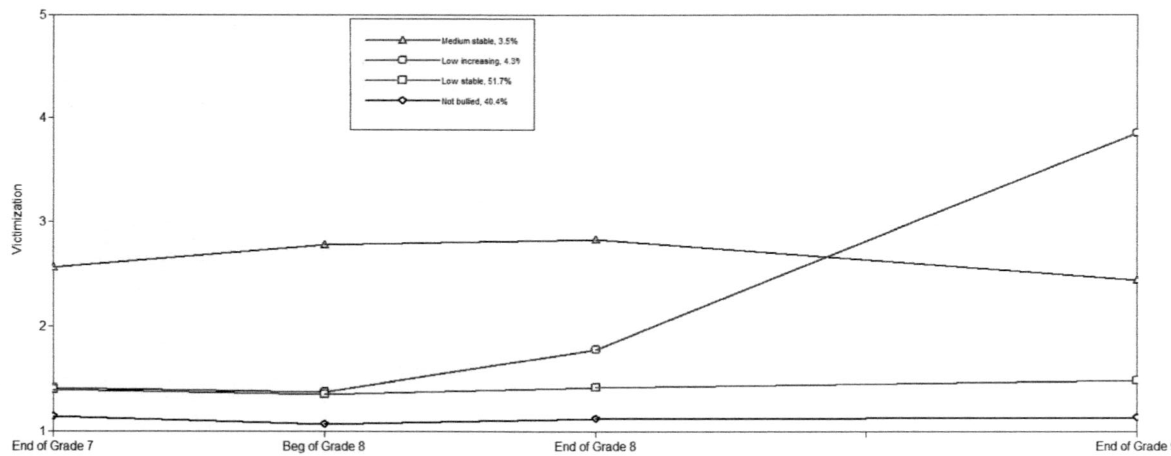

Figure 1. Trajectories of victimization in adolescence ($n = 1810$).

TABLE 1
Types of victimization by gender within victimization trajectories

	End of Grade 7	Beginning of Grade 8	End of Grade 8	End of Grade 9
	Mean(SD)	*Mean(SD)*	*Mean(SD)*	*Mean(SD)*
Males				
Low stable				
Physical	1.18(.40)	1.17(.42)	1.23(.45)	1.27(.63)
Verbal	1.65(.82)	1.50(.82)	1.71(.96)	1.79(1.03)
Relational	1.43(.69)	1.31(.60)	1.46(.76)	1.50(.84)
Low increasing				
Physical	1.15(.32)	1.15(.35)	1.16(.51)*	1.48(.94)
Verbal	1.61(.97)	1.59(.94)	1.79(1.05)	1.90(1.26)
Relational	1.34(.69)	1.39(.88)	1.52(.85)	1.65(1.07)
Medium stable				
Physical	1.06(.15)	1.15(.25)	1.26(.59)	1.19(.69)
Verbal	1.41(.56)	1.45(.79)	1.38(.58)	1.62(1.08)
Relational	1.24(.38)	1.27(.47)	1.42(.74)	1.41(.94)
Not bullied				
Physical	1.23(.53)	1.25(.61)	1.26(.60)	1.41(.88)
Verbal	1.70(.92)	1.61(.95)	1.76(1.03)	1.86(1.16)
Relational	1.49(.79)	1.43(.74)	1.47(.80)	1.53(.93)
Females				
Low stable				
Physical	1.20(.47)	1.15(.38)	1.24(.57)	1.31(.69)
Verbal	1.71(.97)	1.46(.72)	1.75(.98)	1.84(1.08)
Relational	1.51(.81)	1.31(.60)	1.47(.77)	1.59(.89)
Low increasing				
Physical	1.08(.21)	1.08(.15)	1.22(.57)	1.50(.72)
Verbal	1.63(.31)	1.38(.38)	1.96(.86)	2.50(1.30)
Relational	1.38(.43)	1.17(.33)	1.33(.69)	1.63(.53)
Medium stable				
Physical	1.15(.30)	1.17(.24)	1.21(.44)	1.64(1.41)
Verbal	1.63(.47)	1.63(.92)	1.72(.98)	2.03(1.54)
Relational	1.44(.57)	1.25(.55)	1.25(.55)	2.07(1.61)
Not bullied				
Physical	1.19(.45)	1.19(.46)	1.25(.58)	1.31(.79)
Verbal	1.67(.93)	1.52(.80)	1.74(.99)	1.76(1.04)
Relational	1.45(.74)	1.35(.61)	1.49(.79)	1.55(.92)

$^*p < .05$, $^{**}p < .001$.

5.0% respectively) than females (1.4% and 1.9%). Due to the significant differences in distributions, trajectory analyses were conducted separately on the male and female samples. Application of the minimum BIC for model selection did not result in the determination of a clear best model with BIC improving with the addition of groups for both male and female models. The BIC values for two-, three-, four-, and five-group models were compared with the LMR-LRT test of model fit indicating the four-group solution was a better fit than the five-group solution for males ($p = .111$) and a three-group solution was the best fit for females ($p = .132$).

The male victimization trajectories (see Figure 2) followed the original model with the four groups: *not bullied* (32%), *low stable* (56%), *low increasing* (7%), and *stable medium* (5%). For females (see Figure 3) the three victimization trajectory groups consisted of: *not bullied* (37%), *low stable* (57%), and *low increasing* (6%). No high decreasing or high stable trajectory groups were found for males or females. The low stable trajectory corresponds to victimization once or twice in the previous term over the study period; the stable medium trajectory corresponds to victimization every few weeks in the previous term. The low increasing trajectory corresponds to victimization at the end of primary school increasing from once or twice in the previous term to once a week for males at the end of Grade 9 and from once or twice in the previous term to every few weeks for females at the end of Grade 9.

Social health predictors of trajectories of victimization

Loneliness, connectedness to school, peer support, and feeling safe at school were explored as social health predictors of victimization trajectory group membership. The extent to which these social health variables predicted membership to all comparisons of the trajectory groups was assessed.

Loneliness

Males who reported more feelings of loneliness at the end of primary school (Grade 7) had increased odds of being in the low stable, low increasing, and medium stable than the not bullied victimization groups, however loneliness did not differentially predict membership of the three victimization groups. Females who reported more feelings of loneliness were more likely to be in the low stable group than the not bullied group (Table 2), no other differences were found in the likelihood of membership to the groups based on loneliness scores for girls.

Connectedness

Males who felt more connected to school at the end of primary school had reduced odds of being in the medium stable group, whereas females who felt more connected had reduced odds of being in the low stable or low increasing group compared to the not bullied group. Males who reported

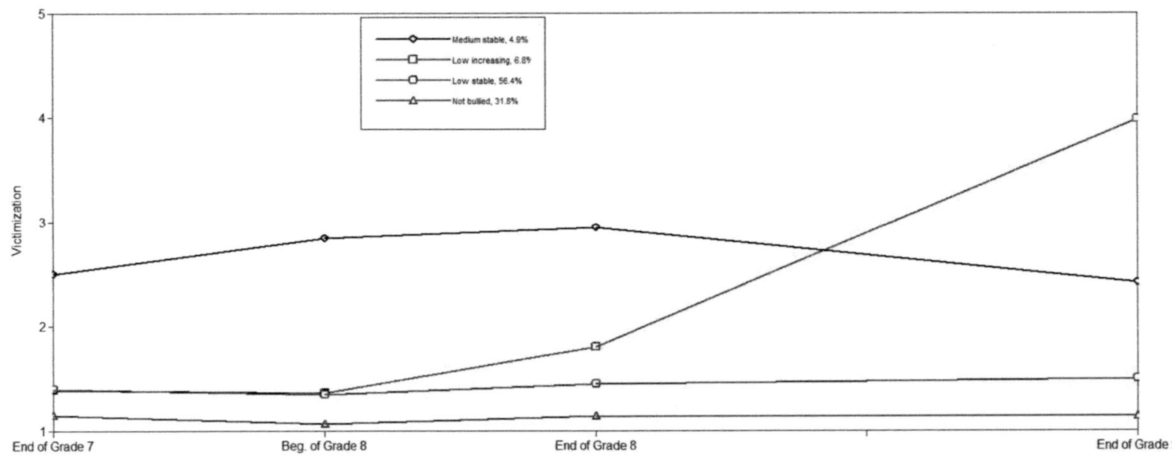

Figure 2. Male trajectories of victimization in adolescence ($n = 881$).

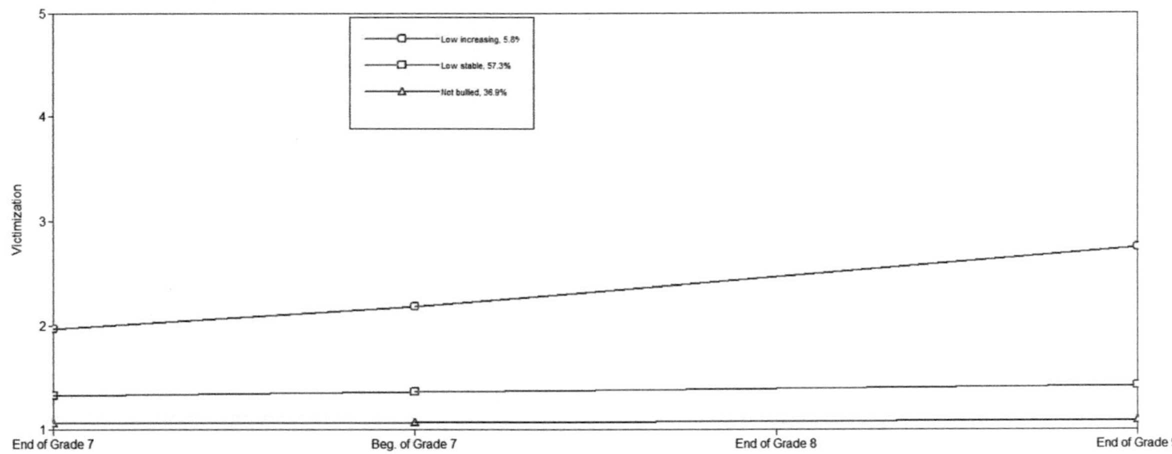

Figure 3. Female trajectories of victimization in adolescence ($n = 927$).

TABLE 2
Multinomial regressions of victimization trajectories on social health measures

OR(95% CI)	*Loneliness*	*Connectedness*	*Peer support*	*Safety at school*
Not bullied reference class				
Males (n=468)				
Medium stable	3.95 (1.71,9.13)**	0.34 (0.19,0.61)**	0.70 (0.20,2.46)	0.24 (0.07,0.81)*
Low increasing	5.48 (2.64,11.39)**	1.26 (0.74,2.13)	1.07 (0.25,4.63)	0.40 (0.15,1.07)
Low stable	3.37 (1.55,7.33) **	0.72 (0.44,1.17)	0.99 (0.36,2.74)	0.44 (0.22,0.88)*
Females (n=543)				
Low increasing	1.70 (0.76,3.80)	0.29 (0.14,0.61)**	0.29 (0.04,1.89)	0.88 (0.24,3.23)
Low stable	1.76 (1.09,2.87)*	0.70 (0.52,0.95)*	0.27 (0.16,0.44)**	0.70 (0.33,1.50)
Low stable reference class				
Males (n=468)				
Medium stable	1.17 (0.68,2.01)	0.48 (0.36,0.65)**	0.70 (0.43,1.16)	0.56 (0.22,1.40)
Low increasing	1.62 (0.70,3.77)	1.76 (1.14,2.70)*	1.08 (0.40,2.92)	0.90 (0.34,2.39)
Females (n=543)				
Low increasing	1.04 (0.38,2.81)	2.43 (1.11,5.31)**	0.94 (0.17,5.34)	0.79 (0.21,3.00)
Low increasing reference class				
Males (n=468)				
Medium stable	0.72 (0.47,1.11)	0.27 (0.16,0.46)**	0.65 (0.31,1.40)	0.62 (0.12,3.07)

Reference trajectory group "Not bullied", $*p < .05$, $**p < .001$. Odds ratio is a measure of the likelihood of class membership; social health measured at beginning of Grade 7; results come from separate models.

less connectedness to school were significantly more likely to be in the medium stable group than in the low increasing and low stable groups, whereas females who reported less connectedness to school were significantly more likely to be in the low increasing than in the low stable group.

Peer support

Peer support was not a predictor of victimization group membership for males. Females who had greater peer support at the end of primary school had reduced odds of being in the low stable group compared to the not bullied group (i.e., were more likely not to be bullied). No other differences were found in the likelihood of membership to the groups based on peer support scores for girls.

Safety at school

Males who felt safe at school at the end of primary school had reduced odds of being in the medium or low stable groups compared to the not bullied group, no other differences were found in the likelihood of membership to the groups based on feelings of safety at school. No significant relationship was found between feeling safe at school and trajectory groups for females.

Victimization trajectories and mental health outcomes

All victimized trajectory groups had significantly higher reported levels of depression and anxiety at the end of Grade 9 compared to the not victimized group. At the end of Grade 7 only males in the stable medium trajectory group had significantly higher levels of depression and anxiety than the not victimized group. At the end of Grade 7, females in the low increasing trajectory group had significantly higher levels of depression and females in the low stable trajectory group had significantly higher levels of anxiety than the not victimized group. Furthermore, males and females in the low increasing victimization groups had higher depression and anxiety scores at the end of Grade 9 than those in the low stable groups (Table 3).

DISCUSSION

This longitudinal study focused on victimization over the transition from primary to the end of the second year of secondary school, a challenging period for adolescents as they experience environmental, physiological, cognitive, and social changes (Barton & Rapkin, 1987). Primary school (Grade 7) social health (loneliness at school, connected to school, peer support, and feeling safe at school) was used to predict victimization trajectory group membership, and victimization trajectory group membership was used to predict mental health outcomes at the end of Grade 9.

Approximately 40% of adolescents in this study experienced no or little victimization at the end of primary school and throughout secondary school with approximately half the students experiencing low stable victimization. A small group of students (4%) reported medium stable levels of victimization from primary through secondary school while a similar proportion were victimized infrequently at the start of secondary school with victimization increasing over the second year of secondary school. Consistent with previous research, the peak for the medium stable group occurred at the beginning of secondary school during the transition from primary to secondary school. In contrast to others who have studied bullying victimization in a younger age group (Boivin et al., 2010; Goldbaum et al., 2003), we did not find high and medium desisting groups or high and medium increasing victimization groups. These differences may be developmental with relational victimization more likely to be experienced during adolescence than physical victimization, as manipulation and aggression are often used as deliberate strategies to

TABLE 3
Tobit regressions of victimization trajectories on mental health outcomes

	Trajectory group			
	Male		*Female*	
Coefficient (95%CI)	*Depression score*	*Anxiety score*	*Depression score*	*Anxiety scores*
Not bullied reference group				
Low stable	0.84 (0.57,1.10)**	0.64 (0.41,0.88)**	0.82 (0.64,1.00)**	0.54 (0.38,0.70)**
Low increasing	2.42 (1.97,2.89)**	2.17 (1.76,2.58)**	1.69 (1.30,2.07)**	1.42 (1.09,1.76)**
Medium stable	1.73 (1.22,2.24)**	1.43 (0.98,1.89)**	–	–
Low increasing reference group				
Low stable	−1.59 (–2.02,–1.17)**	−1.53 (−1.91,−1.15**	−0.89 (−1.23,−0.50)**	−0.88 (−1.20,−0.56)**
Medium stable	−0.70 (–1.30,–0.09)*	−0.74 (−1.28,−0.20)**		
Low stable reference group				
Medium stable	0.90 (1.17,2.02)**	0.79 (0.36,1.22)**		

*$p < 0.05$, **$p < 0.001$. Regression coefficient is estimated difference in depression/anxiety scores between the two trajectory groups being compared; mental health outcomes measured at end of Grade 9.

acquire power and influence, gain dominance and to increase and maintain popularity with peers during this period (LaFontana & Cillessen, 2010; Salmivalli, 2010).

Gender differences were found in both the shape of the trajectories and the number of trajectory groups. As expected, the not bullied and low stable trajectory groups were similar in shape for both males and females. However, females did not report medium stable levels of victimization and the curve for males in the low increasing group was steeper than for females in the same group with the males reporting higher levels of victimization by the end of Grade 9. The severity of victimization in males may indicate higher levels of physical than relational victimization being reported, with adolescent males generally experiencing more direct physical, direct verbal and indirect types of victimization than females (Craig et al., 2009) whereas relational bullying is more common among girls (Nansel et al., 2001). The marked increase in victimization in males implies focused bullying interventions may be needed at the beginning of secondary school.

The social health variables examined in this study as predictors of victimization trajectory groups include loneliness at school, connected to school, peer support, and feeling safe at school. Students who felt lonely at school or less connected to school were more likely to be in stable or increasing victimization groups, whereas feeling safe at school was protective for males while peer support was protective for females. Males who were lonely were most likely to be in the increasing victimization group while males who felt less connected to school were most likely to be in the medium stable group. Females who were lonely were most likely to be in the stable group while females who felt less connected to school were most likely to be in the increasing victimization group. During transition, the ability to make new friends (Akos & Galassi, 2004), the number of friends and quality of friendships (Pellegrini & Bartini, 2000), having friends who are able to help and protect, and being accepted by the peer group are the main social factors identified as protective against victimization (Hodges & Perry, 1996). Victimization has a reciprocal effect on loneliness, with lonely students more likely to be victimized by peers (Berguno, Leroux, McAinsh, & Shaikh, 2004) whereas those victimized are more likely to be lonely, as other peers avoid them for fear of being bullied themselves or losing social status among their peers (Nansel et al., 2001). Confirming prior cross-sectional research where males reported greater perceptions of school safety than females (Brown, Birch, & Vijala, 2005; Varjas, Henrich, & Meyers, 2009), this study found feeling safe at school was a protective factor against victimization for males but not females. Peer support is a factor that can influence feelings of safety at school (Cowie & Oztug, 2008). This is especially the case among female friendships, which are generally fewer in size but stronger than male friendships. In these relationships females generally display greater pro-social and empathetic skills (Bosacki & Wilde Astington, 1999) and place greater importance on social relationships and peer support than males (Smith & Watson, 2004). Findings from this study add to the body of evidence that lonely students are more likely to be victimized.

This longitudinal research supports prior cross-sectional research which found existing relationships between chronic victimization and mental health (Hawker & Boulton, 2000). Importantly, contrary to what was expected, the results of this study show the impact of victimization onset at the start of secondary school has a greater impact on mental health than prolonged victimization. While many students during school transition have to deal with the onset of puberty and the changes in peer relations (and the consequential rise in social stress), in this study the additional effect of onset of victimization is greater than prolonged victimization.

The resulting mental health outcomes of students in the stable and increasing victimization groups highlight the importance of school transition programs which focus on increasing social health and the awareness and prevention of bullying in minimizing harm to students. Prior to and during the primary to secondary school transition period is a critical and opportune time to address student social health. Transition programs can foster school connectedness and feelings of safety at school through a strong school ethos of care, clear social support systems where relationships promote health and well-being and positive classroom management (Cowie, Naylor, Talamelli, Chauhan, & Smith, 2002). Effectively communicating to the school community the school's bullying prevention policy and actions will help to reduce victimization and also increase the students' perceived sense of safety at school, as will increasing adult supervision and enhancing their ability to prevent, detect, and intervene in bullying incidents, and enabling students to support victimized students and easily report bullying (Bradshaw, O'Brennan, & Sawyer, 2008). Peers can reduce bullying by intervening and helping the person being victimized (Salmivalli, 1999) while student, parent, and teacher support can buffer victimized students from internalizing distress (Rigby, 2000). A students' social health can be opportunistically developed in adolescence by modification of the social environment, spending time with pro-social peers and adults, and through targeted skills training.

The prolonged victimization measured in this study is at relatively low levels, measured over a relatively short period of time. While the relationships between social health factors and victimization, and victimization and mental health, can be bi-directional and may already be well established for some students by the time they complete primary school, it is important to examine the predictors of increasing or stable victimization prior to the transition period. Research into victimization measured over a longer period of time would further inform the relationships between social health, victimization, and mental health, and highlight critical times at which to intervene.

Strengths and limitations

There are several strengths of this study. Most importantly, the 2-year (four time points) longitudinal nature of the research design over the transition from primary to secondary school enabled the determination of trajectory groups, social health predictors, and the mental health outcomes at a time that can be socially challenging for most students. Moreover, these findings are robust due to the large sample of students (90%) who completed questionnaires in at least three of the four data collection points. Despite these strengths there are several limitations to this study. First, the use of self-report of social health, victimization, and mental health could result in some of the associations being due to shared method variance. The use of peer, teacher, or parent reports would be useful in examining the relationships further. In addition, the collection of data at home among Grade 7 students was inconsistent with classroom-based data collection procedures used in Grades 8 and 9. To reduce the impact of these differences an explicit and standard protocol (as used in the classroom) was provided to parents for all Grade 7 assessments; however, parents still may have indirectly or directly influenced their children's responses to the questionnaire. While absentee students and those lost to follow-up (approximately 11%) may be more involved in bullying perpetration or victimization behaviors, this potential bias is unlikely to influence the results substantially given the large number of respondents at each data collection. Further, the results may not generalize to the other similar-aged student populations as the sample included only Catholic primary and secondary schools within the Perth metropolitan area. Finally, the trajectory groups were calculated over a relatively short time period (three grade levels) and as such the associations between victimization behaviors, social health, and mental health may have been established prior to the commencement of the study.

CONCLUSION

The impact of chronic victimization on mental health problems in adolescents makes understanding the social health predictors of those within victimization trajectory groups an important priority, especially during transition from primary to secondary school. Adolescents with poorer social health were more likely to be in the increasing and stable trajectory groups than in the not bullied group. Additionally, onset of victimization during transition was associated with poorer mental health outcomes than low stable or no victimization. To enhance the mental health of adolescents, a social health school intervention approach involving primary and secondary schools would help to limit victimization and the harms caused by long-term exposure.

REFERENCES

Akos, P., & Galassi, J. (2004). Middle and high school transitions as viewed by students, parents and teachers. *Professional School Counselling*, *7*(4), 213–221.

Aldwin, C. (2011). Stress and coping across the lifespan. In S. Folkman (Ed.), *The Oxford handbook of stress, health, and coping* (pp. 15–34). New York: Oxford University Press.

Barton, J. H., & Rapkin, B. D. (1987). The transition to junior high school: A longitudinal study of self-esteem, psychological symptomatology, school life, and social support. *Child Development*, *58*(5), 1235–1243.

Berguno, G., Leroux, P., McAinsh, K., & Shaikh, S. (2004). Children's experience of loneliness at school and its relation to bullying and the quality of teacher interventions. *The Qualitative Report*, *9*, 483–499.

Boivin, M., Petitclerc, A., Feng, B., & Barker, E. (2010). The developmental trajectories of peer victimization in middle to late childhood and the changing nature of their behavioral correlates (Report). *Merrill-Palmer Quarterly*, *56*(3), 231–260.

Bond, L., Carlin, J., Thomas, L., Rubin, K., & Patton, G. (2001). Does bullying cause emotional problems? A prospective study of young teenagers. *British Medical Journal*, *323*(7311), 480–484.

Bosacki, S., & Wilde Astington, J. (1999). Theory of mind in preadolescence: Relations between social understanding and social competence. *Social Development*, *8*(2), 237–255.

Bradshaw, C., O'Brennan, L., & Sawyer, A. (2008). Examining variation in attitudes toward aggressive retaliation and perceptions of safety among bullies, victims, and bully/victims. *Professional School Counseling*, *12*, 10–21.

Brown, S., Birch, D., & Vijala, K. (2005). Bullying perspectives: Experiences, attitudes, and recommendations of 9- to 13-year-olds attending health education centers in the United States. *The Journal of School Health*, *75*(10), 384–392.

Carney, J. V. (2008). Perceptions of bullying and associated trauma during adolescence. *Professional School Counseling*, *11*(3), 179, (110).

Cassidy, J., & Asher, S. (1992). Loneliness and peer relations in young children. *Child Development*, *63*(2), 350–365.

Cassidy, T., & Taylor, L. (2005). Coping and psychological distress as a function of the bully victim dichotomy in older children. *Social Psychology of Education*, *8*(3), 249–262.

Cowie, H., Naylor, P., Talamelli, L., Chauhan, P., & Smith, P. (2002). Knowledge, use of and attitudes towards peer support. *Journal of Adolescence*, *25*, 453–467.

Cowie, H., & Oztug, O. (2008). Pupils' perceptions of safety atschool. *Pastoral Care in Education: An International Journal of Personal, Social and Emotional Development*, *26*(2), 59–67.

Craig, W., Harel-Fisch, Y., Fogel-Grinvald, H., Dastaler, S., Hetland, J., & Simons-Morten, B. (2009). A cross-national profile of bullying and victimization among adolescents in 40 countries. *International Journal of Public Health*, *54*, S216–S224.

Cross, D., Hall, M., Waters, S., & Hamilton, G. (2008). A randomised control trial to reduce bullying and other aggressive behaviors in secondary schools. *The Western Australian Health Promotion Foundation.*

Cross, D., Shaw, T., Hearn, L., Epstein, M., Monks, H., Lester, L., & Thomas, L. (2009). Child Health Promotion Research Centre. *Australian covert bullying prevalence study*. Perth: Edith Cowan University.

Ellickson, P., & Hawes, J. (1989). An assessment of active versus passive methods for obtaining parental consent. *Evaluation Review*, *13*, 45–55.

Fekkes, M., Pijpers, F., & Verloove-Vanhorick, S. (2004). Bullying behavior and associations with psychosomatic complaints and depression in victims. *The Journal of Pediatrics*, *144*(1), 17–22.

Garbarino, J. (2001). An ecological perspective on the effects of violence on children. *Journal of Community Psychology*, *29*(3), 361–378.

Goldbaum, S., Craig, W. M., Pepler, D., & Connolly, J. (2003). Developmental trajectories of victimization – Identifying risk and protective factors. *Journal of Applied School Psychology*, *19*(2), 139–156.

Hawker, D., & Boulton, M. (2000). Twenty years' research on peer victimization and psychosocial maladjustment: A meta-analytic review of cross-sectional studies. *Journal of Child Psychology and Psychiatry*, *41*(4), 441–455.

Hodges, E., & Perry, D. (1996). Victims of peer abuse: An overview. *Journal of Emotional and Behavioral Problems*, *5*, 23–28.

Jung, T., & Wickrama, K. (2008). An introduction to latent class growth analysis and growth mixture modeling. *Social and Personality Psychology Compass*, *2*(1), 302–317.

Kaltiala-Heino, R., Rimpela, M., Marttunen, M., Rimpela, A., & Rantanen, P. (1999). Bullying, depression, and suicidal ideation in Finnish adolescents: School survey. *British Medical Journal*, *319*, 348–351.

Kaltiala-Heino, R., Rimpela, M., Rantanen, P., & Rimpela, A. (2000). Bullying at school – an indicator of adolescents at risk for mental disorders. *Journal of Adolescence*, *23*(6), 661–674.

Ladd, G., Kochenderfer, B., & Coleman, C. (1996). Perceptions of peer social support scale. *Child Development*, *67*(3), 1103–1118.

LaFontana, K., & Cillessen, A. (2010). Developmental changes in the priority of perceived status in childhood and adolescence. *Social Development*, *19*(1), 130–147.

Lester, L., Cross, D., Dooley, J., & Shaw, T. (2012a). Bullying victimisation and adolescents: Implications for school based intervention programs, Manuscript submitted for publication.

Lester, L., Cross, D., Dooley, J., & Shaw, T. (2012b). Internalising symptoms: An antecedent or precedent in adolescent peer victimisation. *Australian Journal of Guidance and Counselling*.

Libbey, H. (2004). Measuring student relationships to school: Attachment, bonding, connectedness, and engagement. *Journal of School Health*, *74*(7), 274–283.

Lovibond, S., & Lovibond, P. (1995). Manual for the depression anxiety stress scales. Sydney: Psychology Foundation.

Menesini, E. (2009). Bullying and victimization in adolescence: Concurrent and stable roles and psychological health symptoms. *The Journal of Genetic Psychology*, *170*(2), 115–133.

Menesini, E., Codecasa, E., Benelli, B., & Cowie, H. (2003). Enhancing children's responsibility to take action against bullying: Evaluation of a befriending intervention in Italian middle schools. *Aggressive Behavior*, *29*, 1–14.

Nagin, D. S. (2005). Group-based modeling of development. Cambridge, MA: Harvard University Press.

Nansel, T., Overpeck, M., Pilla, R., Ruan, J., Simons-Morton, B., & Scheidt, P. (2001). Bullying behaviors among US youth: Prevalence and association with psychosocial adjustment. *Journal of the American Medical Association*, *285*(16), 2094–2100.

Naylor, P., & Cowie, H. (1999). The effectiveness of peer support systems in challenging school bullying: The perspectives and experiences of teachers and pupils. *Journal of Adolescence*, *22*, 467–479.

Newman, M. L., Holden, G. W., & Delville, Y. (2005). Isolation and the stress of being bullied. *Journal of Adolescence, 28*(3), 343–357.

Nylund, K., Asparouhov, T., & Muthén, B. (2007). Deciding on the number of classes in Latent Class Analysis and Growth Mixture Modeling: A Monte Carlo simulation study. *Structural Equation Modeling: A Multidisciplinary Journal, 14*(4), 535–569.

O'Brennan, L., Bradshaw, C., & Sawyer, A. (2009). Examining developmental differences in the social-emotional problems among frequent bullies, victims, and bully/victims. *Psychology in the Schools, 46*(2), 100–115.

Olweus, D. (1996). The Revised Olweus Bully/Victim Questionnaire. Bergen, Norway: Mimeo, Research Center for Health Promotion (HEMIL), University of Bergen.

Pellegrini, A. (2002). Bullying, victimisation, and sexual harassment during the transition to middle school. *Educational Psychologist, Volume 37*(3), 151–163.

Pellegrini, A., & Bartini, M. (2000). A longitudinal study of bullying, victimization, and peer affiliation during the transition from primary school to middle school. *American Educational Research Journal, 37*(3), 699–725.

Pepler, D., Jiang, D., Craig, W., & Connolly, J. (2008). Developmental trajectories of bullying and associated factors. *Child Development, 79*(2), 325–338.

Resnick, M., Bearman, P., Blum, R., Bauman, K., Harris, K., Jones, J., ... Udry, J. R. (1997). Protecting adolescents from harm: Findings from the National Longitudinal Study on Adolescent Health. *The Journal of the American Medical Association, 278*(10), 823–832.

Rigby, K. (2000). Effects of peer victimization in schools and perceived social support on adolescent well-being. *Journal of Adolescence, 23*(1), 57–68.

Rigby, K., & Slee, P. (1998). The Peer Relations Questionnaire. Point Lonsdale, VIC: The Professional Reading Guide for Educational Administrators.

Rigby, K., & Slee, P. (1999). Suicidal ideation among adolescent school children, involvement in bully-victim problems, and perceived social support. *Suicide & Life – Threatening Behavior, 29*, 119–130.

Roland, E. (2002). Aggression, depression, and bullying others. *Aggressive Behavior, 28*(3), 198–206.

Rosen, L., Underwood, M., Beron, K., Gentsch, J., Wharton, M., & Rahdar, A. (2009). Persistent versus periodic experiences of social victimization: Predictors of adjustment. *Journal of Abnormal Child Psychology, 37*(5), 693–704.

Salmivalli, C. (1999). Participant role approach to school bullying: Implications for interventions. *Journal of Adolescence, 22*, 453–459.

Salmivalli, C. (2010). Bullying and the peer group: A review. *Aggression and Violent Behavior, 15*, 112–120.

Salmon, G., James, A., Cassidy, E., & Javaloyes, M. (2000). Bullying a review: Presentations to an adolescent psychiatric service and within a school for emotionally and behaviorally disturbed children. *Clinical Child Psychology and Psychiatry, 5*(4), 563–579.

Salmon, G., James, A., & Smith, D. (1998). Bullying in schools: Self reported anxiety, depression, and self esteem in secondary school children. *British Medical Journal, 317*(7163), 924–925.

Smith, P. K. (2004). Bullying: Recent developments. *Child and Adolescent Mental Health*, *9*(3), 98–103.

Smith, P. K., Singer, M., Hoel, H., & Cooper, G. (2003). Victimization in the school and the workplace: Are there any links? *British Journal of Psychology*, *94*(2), 175(114).

Smith, P. K., Talamelli, L., Cowie, H., Naylor, P., & Chauhan, P. (2004). Profiles of non-victims, escaped victims, continuing victims and new victims of school bullying. *British Journal of Educational Psychology*, *74*(4), 565–581.

Smith, P. K., & Watson, D. (2004). An evaluation of the ChildLine in Partnership with Schools (CHIPS) programme. University of London: Unit for School and Family Studies, Goldsmiths College.

Sugden, K., Arseneault, L., Harrington, H., Moffitt, T., Williams, B., & Caspi, A. (2010). The serotonin transporter gene moderates the development of emotional problems among children following bullying victimization. *Journal of American Academy of Child Adolescent Psychiatry*, *49*(8), 830–840.

Sweeting, H., Young, R., West, P., & Der, G. (2006). Peer victimization and depression in early–mid adolescence: A longitudinal study. *British Journal of Educational Psychology*, *76*(3), 577–594.

Underwood, M. K., Beron, K. J., & Rosen, L. H. (2009). Continuity and change in social and physical aggression from middle childhood through early adolescence. *Aggressive Behavior*, *35*(5), 357–375.

Vaillancourt, T., Duku, E., Becker, S., Schmidt, L., Nicol, J., Muir, C., & MacMillian, H. (2011). Peer victimization, depressive symptoms, and high salivary cortisol predict poorer memory in children. *Brain and Cognition*, *77*(2), 191–199.

Varjas, K., Henrich, C. C., & Meyers, J. (2009). Urban middle school students' perceptions of bullying, cyberbullying, and school safety. *Journal of School Violence*, *8*(2), 159–176.

Wothke, W. (1998). Longitudinal and multi-group modeling with missing data. In T. D. Little, K. U. Schnabel, & J. Baumert (Eds.), *Modeling longitudinal and multiple group data: Practical issues, applied approaches and specific examples*. Mahwah, NJ: Lawrence Erlbaum Associates Inc.

Ybarra, M. (2004). Linkages between depressive symptomatology and internet harassment among young regular internet users. *CyberPsychology & Behavior*, *7*(2), 247–258.

Does bullying increase compliance?

Malgorzata Gamian-Wilk
Department of Pedagogies, Psychology Division, University of Lower Silesia, Wroclaw, Poland

Social ostracism can be a form of bullying at the workplace (a process of frequent and repeated acts of hostile communication and humiliation of an employee). Previous findings suggest that experimentally evoked ostracism leads to compliance. The aim of these studies was to examine willingness to comply among bullying targets. It was found that being subjected to bullying is connected with lower proneness to comply with various requests of coworkers (the first study, $N = 197$). A drop in the self-reported compliance rate occurred among those bullied participants who were presented with a description of various types of social exclusion at the workplace (second study, $N = 309$). It is argued that long-term rejection and maltreatment diminishes victims' self-regulation and tendency to fortify threatened needs.

The process when indirect forms of aggression appear repeatedly and systematically against an employee and he or she is unable to defend him or herself from these negative behaviors is called bullying (Einarsen, Hoel, Zapf, & Cooper, 2003). Bullying may develop from personal focused disagreement or a conflict over a specific argument and escalate over time, which means that such negative treatments turn from subtle to more direct and cruel ones (Björkqvist, Osterman, & Hjelt-Back, 1994; Leymann, 1996).

Studies on bullying targets show that they have lowered self-esteem (e.g., Harvey & Keashly, 2003; O'Moore & Kirkham, 2001) and experience anxiety, negative emotionality, depressive symptoms, including suicidal tendencies (Leymann, 1996; Matthiesen & Einarsen, 2004), and stress symptoms (Hoel, Zapf, & Cooper, 2002; Marchand, Demers, & Durand, 2005). Victims feel helpless, and lack a sense of power and control over their situation (Einarsen et al., 2003; Lewis, 2004; Salin, 2003). They report chronic fatigue, problems with concentration, sleeping, and health generally (Hansen et al., 2006; Høgh, Mikkelsen, & Hansen, 2011).

It has been shown that during the process of maltreatment, targets of bullying display a dynamic series of reactions. In Zapf and Gross's (2001) semi-structure interview study, targets declared that as soon as they realized the bad intentions and hostility of a bully, they began with constructive conflict-solving solutions, but the integrating, task-oriented strategies were found to be ineffective (see also Rayner, 1997). Victims tend to resort to other strategies at different stages in the process. Any attempt to find understanding and support at the workplace proves to be ineffective, merely increasing the feeling of shame (Lewis, 2004). Høgh and Dofradottir (2001) found that workers subjected to bullying used humor and avoidance strategies more often and problem solving less often than nonvictims. If there appear any forms of resistance, they are covert because of fear of being punished. In the study by Lutgen-Sandvik (2006), one of the forms of resistance displayed by victims was retaliation. Reciprocation took the form of hostile gossip or fantasies of physically harming or killing the bully. A very common behavior was "talking behind the abuser's back", derogating the bully (Lutgen-Sandvik, 2006). It seems that hostility toward others, which is a kind of reaction of cognitive nature combining a sense of resentment and suspicions (Palmer & Thakordas, 2005), is one of the responses of victims of bullying to maltreatment (Gamian-Wilk, Bjørkelo, & Hauge, in preparation, (2013); Ireland & Archer, 2002). It seems that bullying as a process of long-lasting maltreatment and rejection results in experiencing stress and impairment in many areas including social functioning: it is difficult for a victim to respond with pro-social behaviors when having to bear constant humiliation.

WORKPLACE OSTRACISM AS ONE OF THE NEGATIVE BULLYING ACTIVITIES

Bullying is interpersonal by nature and social isolation has been regarded as one of the most frequent forms of negative activities reported by victims and differentiated in empirical studies (e.g., Einarsen, 2000; Leymann, 1996; Vartia, 1993), although bullying is a broader construct that can involve personal bullying (making insulting remarks, excessive teasing, spreading gossip or rumors, persistent criticism, and isolating), work-related bullying (excessive monitoring of work, assigning unreasonable deadlines and unmanageable workloads, assigning meaningless tasks, or no tasks at all), and physical intimidation (various forms of threatening, physical abuse) (Einarsen et al., 2011). It has been demonstrated that ostracism is a common experience in the workplace context and may have different forms: being ignored at work, being unanswered when giving greetings, being left alone during lunch breaks, not being looked at, being shut out during conversation, or not being invited for informal meetings (Ferris, Brown, Berry, & Liam, 2008). In a survey conducted by Fox and Stallworth (2005), it was found that 66% of workers had experienced being ignored or rejected during the past 5 years. Although ostracism has been perceived as one of the core bullying activities and causes similar devastating consequences, research has shown that workplace ostracism per se is conceptually separate from bullying (Ferris et al., 2008).

Workplace ostracism often aims at expelling a victim from the workplace community (Einarsen et al., 2003). This is an extreme form of social rejection but ostracism is also represented by more subtle behaviors, e.g., using silent treatment or avoiding eye contact (Williams, 2007). Ostracism, which leaves a feeling of being invisible or of not existing, communicates symbolically to the target that he or she is dead and meaningless for the source (Williams, 2007). Therefore, even short episodes of social rejection lead to immediate negative consequences, such as hurt feelings (distress, anger, sadness) and threat to social self-esteem, need of belonging, need of control, and sense of meaningful existence (Smart Richman & Leary, 2009; Williams & Zadro, 2005; Zadro, Williams, & Richardson, 2004). These emotional responses occur immediately after rejection, but behaviors which accompany these reactions vary considerably, from socially desirable to withdrawal or antisocial responses. Smart Richman and Leary (2009) in a multimotive theory provide a conceptual framework explaining different outcomes to various kinds of rejection circumstances. Socially appealing responses are possible if exclusion is connected with high perceived costs, if one expects that a relationship may be repaired or if a relationship is highly valued. Conversely, in the case of such chronic rejection as workplace bullying where victims perceive the exclusion as unfair and have no hope of repairing the relations, they tend to behave aggressively or they withdraw (e.g., Maner, DeWall, Baumeister, & Schaller, 2007; Twenge, 2005; Williams, 2007; Williams & Zadro, 2005). Therefore, it is reasonable to predict that long-term bullying should reduce people's tendencies to respond to rejection in a pro-social manner.

SOCIAL EXCLUSION AND COMPLIANCE

In general, if possible, people seek acceptance and tend to restore their positive self-esteem and sense of belonging after rejection by behaving in a socially desirable way, e.g., by engaging in a collective task rather than in an individual task (Williams & Sommer, 1997), conforming to others (Williams, Cheung, & Choi, 2000) or mimicking other persons' behavior (Lakin & Chartrand, 2005). In line with these findings, Carter-Sowell, Chen, and Williams (2008) demonstrated that regardless of the tactic employed (the foot-in-the-door, the door-in-the-face, and/or a single target request), experimentally evoked ostracism increased compliance. It is therefore important to deepen the knowledge on the link between being ostracized and susceptibility to social influence in the context of real-life situations. The aim of this study was to investigate whether long-term social exclusion in the form of bullying an individual leads to his or her compliance.

It seems therefore that the bullying phenomenon may represent boundary conditions, that is, circumstances in which anti-social rather than socially desirable responses are more likely to occur after exclusion. As compliance is perceived as a socially desirable behavior displayed after being ostracized (Carter-Sowell et al., 2008), a drop in compliance among bullying targets was predicted. As in the Carter-Sowell et al. study (2008), it was shown that rejection leads to greater compliance rates regardless of the social influence technique used; it is reasonable to hypothesize that bullying victims will not be compliant with single requests. Therefore, the first hypothesis stated that *being bullied at work would result in lower proneness to comply in comparison with not being bullied situation* (H1). It was also predicted that *the drop in the tendency to comply would be even greater among bullied workers after remembering being exposed to ostracism by other coworkers* (H1a). As it was earlier proved experimentally, evoked ostracism resulted in greater compliance. It was anticipated that *the mere memory of being exposed to ostracism at work would result in increased proneness to comply* (H2). In previous studies, it was shown that both experimentally evoked ostracism and being rejected at the workplace cause a significant drop in needs satisfaction and mood. Thus, the third hypothesis stated that *being subjected to bullying at the workplace would lead to lower needs satisfaction and lowered mood* (H3). Moreover, it was predicted that *the drop in needs satisfaction and mood would be even greater among bullied targets after remembering being exposed to ostracism by other coworkers* (H3a). Finally, it was anticipated that *the mere memory of being exposed to ostracism at work would result in a decrease in needs satisfaction and mood* (H4).

To test these predictions, one questionnaire study and one quasi-experimental study were conducted. In the first study, only the first hypothesis was tested. The second study verified all of the four predictions.

STUDY 1

Overview

The first study aimed at investigating the level of compliance among bullying victims. Participants representing various professions completed two questionnaires: the Negative Acts Questionnaire to diagnose bullying symptoms and the Compliance Scale measuring the general tendency to agree to requests asked by coworkers.

Procedure and sample

The study was conducted among 197 employees, recruited among mature part-time university students taking a further education course in pedagogy. The study was an integrated part of an academic course and participants were not rewarded for their cooperation. The selection criteria were that the participants were in full-time positions and in contact with their superiors or subordinates at least three times a week (recruitment procedure is according to Glasø & Einarsen, 2008).

The participants' age range was from 20 to 51 ($M = 26.13$, SD $= 6.22$) and 81% of the sample were female. Nineteen participants were leaders and the others were subordinates. The majority of the participants worked in the public sector (76%), mainly in education (37%) and health services (26%).

Instruments

Bullying

Workplace bullying was measured by two different methods. First, workplace bullying was measured by a Polish version of the Negative Acts Questionnaire – Revised (NAQ-R) (Warszewska-Makuch, 2007), developed by Einarsen, Hoel, and Notelaers (2009). The NAQ-R consists of 22 items and describes different behaviors which may be perceived as bullying or harassment if they occur on a regular basis. All items are formulated in behavioral terms, with no reference to the phrase "bullying and harassment." The NAQ-R contains items referring to both direct (e.g., open attack) and indirect (social isolation, slander) behavior. It also contains items referring to personal as well as work-related forms of bullying. For each item, the respondents were asked how often they had been exposed to the behavior at their present workplace during the last 6 months. Response categories were (1) "never," (2) "now and then," (3) "monthly," (4) "weekly," and (5) "daily." The NAQ-R showed good internal consistency in the present study (Cronbach's $\alpha = .92$).

After the NAQ-R was listed in the questionnaire, the respondents were asked to indicate whether they had been exposed to bullying at work during the last 6 months according to a formal definition of bullying at work (see Einarsen & Skogstad, 1996). The response categories were (1) "No," (2) "Yes, but occasionally," (3) "Yes, now and then," (4) "Yes, once a week," and (5) "Yes, several times a week."

Groups of bullying targets ($N = 32$) and nonvictims ($N = 30$) were distinguished on the basis of Leymann's criteria (one has to be exposed to at least one negative act per week over a period of at least 6 months to be considered as a bullying target)[1] on the sum of 22 NAQ-R items.

[1] Although the NAQ (NAQ-R) results of individual items may be summed and the sum scores may be included in correlation analyses or regression analyses, the behavioral experience approach may also be used to distinguish between different groups of respondents (targets and nontargets). The common method of separating targets from nonvictims is to apply an operational criterion (Nielsen, Notelaers, & Einarsen, 2011). This approach seems to fit most to the theory of the bullying phenomenon which is not a "continuous" experience but a phenomenon of several criteria (e.g., Leymann, 1996). It is, therefore, more reasonable to separate victims from nonvictims. On the other hand, the operational criterion has several limitations. Nielsen et al. (2011) recommend latent class cluster analysis as the best method of identifying different groups of respondents (e.g., personal bullying victims, work-related bullying victims, and occasional victims). The purpose of this study was to compare the strategies of workers being bullied (according to the definition) and not bullied.

Compliance

The Compliance Scale consisted of 15 items connected with agreeing to requests proposed by supervisors or coworkers. It contains items referring to both task-related (e.g., performing some additional duty, explaining work problems, and borrowing money) and social (e.g., spending time with colleagues) requests. In some statements, the difficulty or irrationality of requests is stressed. For each item, the respondents were asked to what extent they agreed with a particular request. Response categories were (1) "does not describe me," (2) "rather does not describe me well," (3) "hard to say," (4) "describes me rather well," and (5) "describes me well."

Factor analysis of the data obtained in the first study using Principal Axis Factoring and Promax rotation with Kaiser nominalization revealed two meaningful factors: compliance with task-related requests (11 items, e.g., "I agree to do a task which is not my duty when a work mate asks me to") and compliance with social requests (four items, e.g., "I agree to go for a lunch with my friends when they invite me even if I do not have time"). The total percentage of variance for the two factors was 62.18% (54.91% of variance for task-related requests and 7.28% for social requests). The initial eigenvalues were, respectively, 8.24 and 1.09. The task-related compliance scale showed good internal consistency in the present study (Cronbach's $\alpha = .93$). The social compliance scale showed satisfactory consistency (Cronbach's $\alpha = .83$). Both task-related and social compliance scales were highly correlated, $r = .74$, $p < .001$, $d = 2.20$. Reliability of the total compliance scale was Cronbach's $\alpha = .94$.

RESULTS

Table 1 shows descriptive statistics for bullying, the total score of the compliance scale, task-related compliance, and social compliance. The hypothesis which stated that bullying targets would report a low level of compliance was confirmed: bullying targets were generally less compliant, both with social and task-related requests (Table 2).

TABLE 1
Descriptive statistics for negative activities, compliance in general, task-related compliance, and social compliance

	M	*SD*	*Min*	*Max*
Negative acts	40.09	15.77	22	103
Compliance (total score)	33.07	13.72	15	71
Task-related compliance	24.38	10.65	11	51
Social compliance	8.69	3.83	4	20

TABLE 2
Differences in general, task-related, and social compliance between bullying targets and nonvictims

	Bullying targets		*Nontargets*				
	M	*SD*	*M*	*SD*	*t*	*p*	*Hedges g*
Compliance	26.59	10.11	36.93	13.89	3.33	.002	.84
Task-related compliance	19.03	7.63	27.37	10.49	3.59	.001	.90
Social compliance	7.56	3.43	9.57	3.87	2.15	.04	.54

DISCUSSION

In general, the results confirm the main prediction (H1): being subjected to negative treatment at work is connected with low compliance with various requests of coworkers. These results suggest that although single acts of ostracism, as shown in experimental designs (Carter-Sowell et al., 2008), lead to compliance as a sign of socially desirable behavior, long-term rejection results in completely opposite responses. Bullied participants were reluctant to agree to both task-related and social requests: they tended to refuse to do additional work, stay extra hours, lend money or personal things, give work materials and also spend time with work mates, have lunch with them, or go for informal meetings. If they have no time or they have other urgent duties, they do not decide to comply with coworkers' requests. On the one hand, such responses appear to be assertive and reflexive. However, being reluctant to agree to colleagues' requests means not meeting social expectations and may result in further exclusion.

These findings are in line with Smart Richman and Leary's (2009) multimotive model of reactions to rejection: long-lasting ostracism at the workplace assessed as an unpleasant experience leads to a drop in socially desirable behaviors. The results are also consistent with data suggesting that bullying victims tend to withdraw rather than to cope constructively in the long term (e.g., Zapf & Gross, 2001). Moreover, research on bullying targets' profile indicates that employees who have been exposed to bullying at work lack social competence (Matthiesen & Einarsen, 2001, 2004), are less social and talkative, as well as less likeable, understanding, and diplomatic (Glasø, Matthiesen, Nielsen, & Einarsen, 2007; Lind, Glasø, Pallesen, & Einarsen, 2009).

However, it is highly possible that it is not the victims' personality features but the process of workplace ostracism and maltreatment which generates bullying targets' socially undesirable responses. Unfortunately, research has shown that social rejection deteriorates self-regulation, which is connected with a significant drop in cognitive functioning, and lower resistance to temptations (Baumeister & Dewall, 2005). Worsened self-regulation may result in limited capacities of proper social functioning. As Baumeister and Dewall (2005) state, many people experience a downward spiral in which social exclusion may lead to socially disvalued behavior which may, in turn, elicit further rejection. Bullying victims' poorer self-regulation caused by social exclusion may constitute a pitfall: it seems extremely difficult to escape from the downward spiral and regain social acceptance.

It is, however, important to ponder whether bullying targets have suitable opportunities to agree to coworkers' requests. In the workplace where bullying flourishes, that is, in a climate of conflicts, fear, and low job satisfaction, social interactions may be deteriorated (Hauge, Skogstad, & Einarsen, 2007). It seems difficult to be compliant with coworkers who bully or do not provide support. Victims are often left alone, isolated, which means they do not receive any requests. Therefore, by having no possibilities to be compliant, they may have no chances to fulfill their threatened needs and to regain social acceptance.

Moreover, the decrease in compliance rate may not be a result of social exclusion as being bullied means not only being rejected from a group but also being a subject of gossip, negative communication, work overload, and other forms of maltreatment. In the second study, it was assessed whether the rejection itself causes a decrease in needs satisfaction and mood and a drop in compliance. In this study, participants declared their compliance with requests of coworkers staying at the University, which is in a quite different context from their workplaces. It is possible that being in an alternative group distant from unpleasant work conditions influenced the results. In the second study, the context of workplace has been highlighted.

STUDY 2

Overview

The aim of the second study was to highlight the context of workplace rejection. To meet this purpose, after completing the questionnaire concerning being bullied at work, employees did a recall task of being either included or excluded by their coworkers. Then they completed the measure of compliance, manipulation check, and a questionnaire measuring the level of satisfying needs and the level of mood index.

Procedure and sample

The study was conducted among 309 employees, recruited among mature part-time university students taking a further education course in pedagogies, special pedagogies, banking, management, finance, and marketing. The study was an integrated part of an academic course and participants were not rewarded for their cooperation. The selection criteria were the same as in the first study.

The participants' age range was from 21 to 48 ($M = 27.64$, SD $= 6.18$) and 69% of the sample were female. Eighty-six participants were leaders and the rest were subordinates. The majority of the participants worked in the public sector (69%), in education, health services, social care sector, production, trade, administration, finance, banking, police, prisons, and nonprofit organizations.

Instruments

Bullying

Polish version of the NAQ-R (Warszewska-Makuch, 2007) described in the first study was used. The NAQ-R showed good internal consistency in the present study (Cronbach's $\alpha = .94$). Groups of bullying targets ($N = 48$) and nonvictims ($N = 46$) were distinguished on the basis of Leymann's criteria on the sum of 22 NAQ-R items.

Exclusion versus inclusion at workplace

Participants were asked to think about their workplace. Previous research has shown that recall and re-living procedures occurred to be successful in generating negative ostracism consequences (Chen, Williams, Fitness, & Newton, 2008; Craighead, Kimball, & Rehak, 1979). In the *exclusion* condition it was stated that in each organization coworkers sometimes neglect or reject others either in delegating tasks, passing messages, inviting for meetings, or by not answering phones or emails. Participants were to remember and describe situations from their own work when other coworkers ostracized them in any way. In the *inclusion* condition, it was stated that in each organization coworkers sometimes invite each other to participate in collective tasks or meetings, become involved in spreading messages, and answer emails or phones immediately. Participants were to remember and describe situations from their own work when other coworkers included them in any way.

Compliance

The compliance scale described in the first study was used. On the basis of factor analysis of the data obtained in the second study using Principal Axis Factoring extraction and Promax rotation with Kaiser nominalization, it was decided to treat the compliance scale as a homogeneous measure (although factor analysis revealed four factors with initial eigenvalues of 5.26, 1.45, 1.37, and 1.15, the factor loadings in the first factor were not lower than .62, whereas in two others they were lower than .43; the scree plot indicated one significant factor explaining 35.05% of variance, whereas the other three factors explained 9.67%, 9.15%, and 7.65% of variance; and analysis of the three other factors' items did not show any logical structure). The compliance scale showed good internal consistency in this study (Cronbach's $\alpha = .92$).

Fundamental needs and mood

After describing being excluded or included at the workplace and completing the compliance scale, participants were asked to provide self-reports concerning their satisfaction levels with belonging, self-esteem, meaningful existence, and control on 7-point scales (after van Beest & Williams, 2006; Cronbach's $\alpha = .82$ in this study). Next they were asked to assess their emotional state at work also on 7-point scales. This mood index contained three items assessing positive emotions and three items assessing negative emotions (after van Beest & Williams, 2006; Cronbach's $\alpha = .82$ in this study). Negative emotions were reverse-scored. Both needs satisfaction and mood items referred to workplace context: participants were to evaluate the level of their needs fulfillment and mood at their workplace. Finally, to check the exclusion versus inclusion manipulation, participants were asked in three items on a 7-point scale to evaluate the extent to which (a) people in general are ostracized (one item) and (b) they themselves feel rejected by their coworkers (three items on 7-point scales) (in accordance with van Beest & Williams, 2006; Cronbach's $\alpha = .73$). It was also checked whether participants after reading the manipulation message described any situation.

At the end of the study, all of the participants were thanked and debriefed.

RESULTS

Manipulation check

The manipulation was found to be successful. An (inclusion vs. exclusion manipulation) analysis of variance (ANOVA) on the sum of three items measuring the level of feeling rejected and ignored at the workplace showed that participants who were to remember and describe the situation of being rejected at their workplace felt significantly more rejected, $F\ (1{,}307) = 6.15$, $p = .01$, $\eta_p^2 = .02$. The fact that participants described a situation after remembering being included or excluded at the workplace influenced the manipulation check results, increasing the effect. A 2 (inclusion vs. exclusion manipulation) × 2 (described a situation vs. did not describe any situation) (ANOVA) on the sum of three items measuring the level of feeling being rejected at the workplace indicated a main effect of manipulation, $F\ (1{,}119) = 12.15$, $p < .001$, $\eta_p^2 = .04$, a main effect of description, $F\ (1{,}57) = 6.13$, $p = .01$, $\eta_p^2 = .02$, and an interaction effect, $F\ (1{,}57) = 4.79$, $p = .03$, $\eta_p^2 = .02$. Therefore, although only 120 participants described their own experiences of being included (85 participants) or excluded (35 participants) at the workplace, still merely reading the information was found to have an impact on the feeling of being included or rejected at work, respectively, to the manipulation information.[2]

Means and standard deviations of the compliance index, needs satisfaction, and mood are given in Table 3.

Compliance rates

A 2 (inclusion vs. exclusion manipulation) × 2 (bullied vs. not bullied) ANOVA on compliance yielded a main effect of being bullied, F (1,89) = 16.08, $p < .01$, $\eta_p^2 = .16$, a main effect of exclusion manipulation F (1,89) = 6.18, $p = .02$, $\eta_p^2 = .07$, and a significant interaction effect, F (1,89) = 14.16, $p = .001$, $\eta_p^2 = .14$ (Figure 1).

The analysis of contrasts indicated that there is a significant difference in proneness to comply between bullying targets and nontargets in the inclusion condition (F (1,89) = 36.91, $p < .001$, $\eta_p^2 = .42$). The difference was not significant in the exclusion condition (F (1,89) = .03, $p = .87$).

This result suggests that although remembering a single situation of being ostracized at work produces compliance among nonvictims, it seems that it may not be the situation of exclusion itself which causes a drop in compliance among bullying victims. To investigate the possible predictors of compliance, further analysis of contrasts among nonvictims and among victims comparing needs satisfaction, mood, and feeling of being excluded as predictors (dichotomized based on median split) on compliance was conducted. It was found that only mood was a significant predictor of compliance (F (1,24) = 7.56, $p = .01$, $\eta_p^2 = .25$).

In conclusion, although in the second study bullying targets were generally less reluctant to comply with coworkers' requests (H1 was only partially confirmed), they were less willing to comply after focusing on an exclusion situation at work (H1a has been confirmed). H2 has been confirmed: the mere focusing on a situation of being rejected at work produces greater proneness to comply among nonvictims.

Fundamental needs

A 2 (inclusion vs. exclusion manipulation) × 2 (bullied vs. not bullied) ANOVA on needs yielded only a strong main effect of being bullied, F (1,93) = 86.34, $p < .001$, $\eta_p^2 = .49$, such that nonbullied participants had much more satisfied

[2] Approximately 40% of the narratives ($N = 48$) were selected randomly and subjected to a word count. There were no significant differences in the number of words participants wrote between included ($M = 22.82$, SD = 20.27) and excluded ($M = 30.13$, SD = 20.26) conditions, $t = 1.27$, $p = .21$. The narratives contained mainly descriptions of facts. Single participants who were to remember situations when they were included at work stated the consequences (positive emotions, relationships deepened).

TABLE 3

Descriptive statistics for negative activities, compliance, positive and negative emotions, and fundamental needs

	Overall descriptives				*Inclusion condition*				*Exclusion condition*			
	M	*SD*	*Min*	*Max*	*M*	*SD*	*Min*	*Max*	*M*	*SD*	*Min*	*Max*
Negative acts	36.28	14.15	22	106	35.94	14.69	22	106	36.80	13.86	22	82
Compliance	44.41	10.48	15	70	44.19	10.51	15	70	44.66	10.47	12	70
Emotions index	30.66	6.34	10	42	31.11	6.28	10	42	30.14	6.42	11	42
Belongingness	27.47	5.62	14	36	28.02	5.67	14	36	26.75	5.51	15	35
Self-esteem	26.39	5.20	10	35	26.27	4.75	16	35	26.45	5.68	10	35
Control	22.89	6.45	8	51	22.95	6.32	8	35	22.72	6.61	8	51
Meaningful existence	28.37	5.38	13	35	28.67	5.25	15	35	28.00	5.55	13	35
Need satisfaction index	105.4	17.06	68	140	106.46	15.83	72	140	103.92	18.24	68	140

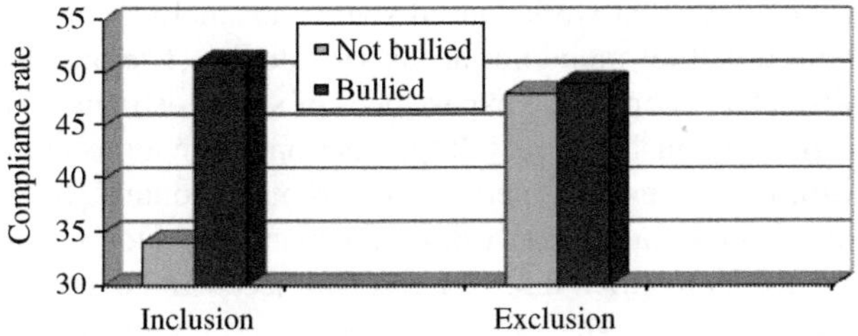

Figure 1. The influence of inclusion versus exclusion manipulation and being bullied at the workplace on compliance.

needs ($M = 112.52$, SD = 14.74) than bullied participants ($M = 86.94$, SD = 18.37).

Mood

A 2 (inclusion vs. exclusion manipulation) × 2 (bullied vs. not bullied) ANOVA on mood yielded only a strong main effect of being bullied, F (1,93) = 83.54, $p < .001$, $\eta_p^2 = .51$, such that nonbullied participants were much more positive ($M = 36.36$, SD = 3.68) than bullied participants ($M = 24.52$, SD = 6.51).

In conclusion, H3 has been confirmed: bullied participants experienced lower levels of needs satisfaction and mood at the workplace. Moreover, H3a has not been confirmed: bullying targets did not display lower mood when focused on being excluded at work. However, although the manipulation of focusing on inclusion versus exclusion at work was successful, H4 was not confirmed: reading information about possibilities of being rejected or included by a group and remembering such situations influenced neither mood nor needs satisfaction regarding work context.

GENERAL DISCUSSION

Previous research has shown that experimentally evoked ostracism leads to greater compliance rates (Carter-Sowell et al., 2008). Greater compliance after ostracism was due to lowered needs satisfaction. The aim of this study was to check whether this pattern of results would be replicated in the context of long-term workplace rejection.

First of all, the pattern of results obtained by Carter-Sowell et al. (2008) has been confirmed in the second study: even the mere focus on social exclusion produces greater compliance. Consistent with other studies, the threat of being rejected is information which generates socially valuable responses (e.g., Lakin & Chartrand, 2005; Williams & Sommer, 1997). Here, reading the examples of social ostracism at the workplace was a sufficient threat to generate counteraction and report being more compliant. Surprisingly, although reading a message pointing out various kinds of social exclusion at work caused significant feelings of being rejected at work, it decreased neither mood nor needs satisfaction. The possible explanation of these results is that such single experiences of social ostracism at work did not impact on the participants' general job satisfaction as the items in the mood index and needs fulfillment referred generally to workplace context. It is even possible that participants' immediate socially desirable responses such as compliance with work mates' requests fortified threatened social needs and even resulted in more positive emotionality. Maybe if asked about certain episodes of rejection, participants would report lowered mood and needs satisfaction (if a particular experience of ostracism caused negative emotionality and threatened needs), which would mediate compliance. These suggestions need to be examined further.

Most importantly, the present studies are the first studies investigating compliance among bullying targets. The first study has shown that being subjected to workplace bullying is connected with unwillingness to comply with both task-related and social requests of coworkers. The second study has proven that being bullied causes a dramatic drop in needs satisfaction and mood. Moreover, being bullied leads to a lower level of compliance, but only after focusing on the situations of being excluded at work. The findings obtained in both studies are therefore consistent.

Interestingly, it was neither the feeling of being excluded nor lowered needs satisfaction which was found to predict compliance among bullying targets. Victims' compliance was explained only by lowered mood. Perhaps it is not social exclusion which is so harmful and, therefore, decreases the willingness to perform socially desirable behaviors but there may be other negative activities of coworkers which result in targets' negative emotionality and unwillingness to comply and to affiliate with others.

Second, the findings suggest that in the case of bullying targets, the threat of social exclusion is not a motivation to undertake socially desirable behaviors. As social ostracism indicates that one has not behaved in a socially valuable way, nonvictims seem to respond to this cue and change their behavior. On the contrary, victims' responses are much less differentiated than nonvictims' reactions to inclusion or exclusion information. Bullying targets appear not to take advantage of such a social cue as exclusion to self-regulate and display socially desirable behavior.

Future studies should focus on replicating the obtained results using behavior-based compliance measures as it is traditionally evoked and observed (e.g., Pratkanis, 2007). Like in other fields of bullying research (Monks & Coyne, 2011), it is important to implement various methods of assessing both negative workplace activities and targets' responses. In this study, compliance was diagnosed by self-reports, which is very common in workplace bullying research (implementing surveys, questionnaires, or semi-structured interviews). Behavior observation or in-depth case studies are rather rarely conducted.

In this study, bullying was evaluated outside of the workplace, which is to some extent beneficial. Participants could freely and safely answer questions without being afraid of being punished. We may assume that self-report measures are more credible when completed outside the workplace. However, future studies should take organizational context (climate, values, and leadership) into account. Bullying at work is a complex phenomenon which develops over time. There are a number of organizational, group, and individual antecedents promoting bullying (Coyne, 2011). Moreover, responses of bullying victims to negative activities should be analyzed in the larger context of time. Future studies should focus on investigating the sources and dynamics of bullying targets' compliance.

REFERENCES

Baumeister, R. F., & Dewall, C. N. (2005). The inner dimension of social exclusion: Intelligent thought and self-regulation among rejected persons. In K. D. Williams, J. P. Forgas & W. von Hippel (Eds.), *The social outcast: Ostracism, social exclusion, rejection, and bullying* (pp. 53–73). New York, Hove: Psychology Press.

Björkvist, K., Osterman, K., & Hjelt-Back, M. (1994). Aggression among university employees. *Aggressive Behavior, 20*, 173–184.

Carter-Sowell, A. R., Chen, Z., & Williams, K. D. (2008). Ostracism increases social susceptibility. *Social Influence, 3*, 143–153.

Chen, Z., Williams, K. D., Fitness, J., & Newton, N. C. (2008). When hurt won't heal: Exploring the capacity to relive social pain. *Psychological Science, 19*, 789–795.

Coyne, I. (2011). Bullying in the workplace. In C. P. Monks & I. Coyne (Eds.), *Bullying in different contexts* (pp. 157–184). Cambridge: Cambridge University Press.

Craighead, W. E., Kimball, W. H., & Rehak, P. J. (1979). Mood changes, physiological responses, and self-statement during social rejection imaginery. *Journal of Personality and Social Psychology, 53*, 1024–1037.

Einarsen, S. (2000). Harassment and bullying at work: A review of the Scandinavian approach. *Aggression and Violent Behavior, 5*, 379–401.

Einarsen, S., Hoel, H., & Notelaers, G. (2009). Measuring exposure to bullying and harassment at work: Validity, factor structure and psychometric properties of the Negative Acts Questionnaire – Revised. *Work and Stress, 23*, 24–44.

Einarsen, S., Hoel, H., Zapf, D., & Cooper, C. L. (2003). The concept of bullying at work: The European tradition. In S. Einarsen, H. Hoel, D. Zapf & C. L. Cooper (Eds.), *Bullying and emotional abuse in the workplace: International perspectives in research and practice*. New York, NY: Taylor & Francis.

Einarsen, S., Hoel, H., Zapf, D., & Cooper, C. L. (2011). The concept of bullying and harassment at work: The European tradition. In S. Einarsen, H. Hoel, D. Zapf & C. L. Cooper (Eds.), *Bullying and harassment in the workplace: Developments in theory, research, and practice* (pp. 3–40). Boca Raton, London, New York: Taylor & Francis Press.

Einarsen, S., & Skogstad, A. (1996). Bullying at work: Epidemiological findings in public and private organizations. *European Journal of Work and Organizational Psychology, 5*, 185–201.

Ferris, D. L., Brown, D. J., Berry, J. W., & Lian, H. (2008). The development and validation of the workplace ostracism scale. *Journal of Applied Psychology, 93*, 1348–1366.

Fox, S., & Stallworth, L. E. (2005). Racial/ethnic bullying: Exploring links between bullying and racism in the US workplace. *Journal of Vocational Behavior, 66*, 438–456.

Gamian-Wilk, M., Bjørkelo, B., & Hauge, L. J. (Manuscript in preparation, 2013). The role of personality in the form of temperament in relation to bullying at work.

Glasø, L., & Einarsen, S. (2008). Emotion regulation in leader-follower relationships. *European Journal of Work and Organizational Psychology, 17*, 482–500.

Glasø, L., Matthiesen, S. B., Nielsen, M. B., & Einarsen, S. (2007). Do targets of workplace bullying portray a general victim personality profile? *Scandinavian Journal of Psychology, 48*, 313–319.

Hansen, A. M., Høgh, A., Persson, R., Karlson, B., Gerde, A. H., & Ørbæk, P. (2006). Bullying at work, health outcomes, and physiological stress response. *Journal of Psychosomatic Research, 60*, 63–72.

Harvey, S., & Keashly, L. (2003). Predicting the risk for aggression in the workplace: Risk factors, self-esteem and time at work. *Social Behavior and Personality, 31*, 807–814.

Hauge, L. J., Skogstad, A., & Einarsen, S. (2007). Relationships between stressful work environment and bullying: Results of a large representative study. *Work & Stress, 21*, 220–242.

Hoel, H., Zapf, D., & Cooper, C. L. (2002). Workplace bullying and stress. *Historical and Current Perspectives on Stress and Health, 2*, 293–333.

Høgh, A., & Dofradottir, A. (2001). Coping with bullying in the workplace. *European Journal of Work and Organizational Psychology, 10*, 485–495.

Høgh, A., Mikkelsen, E. G., & Hansen, A. M. (2011). Individual consequences of bullying/ mobbing. In S. Einarsen, H. Hoel, D. Zapf & C. L. Cooper (Eds.), *Bullying and harassment in the workplace. Development in theory, research, and practice*. London, New York: Taylor & Francis Press.

Ireland, J. L., & Archer, J. (2002). The perceived consequences of responding to bullying with aggression: A study of male and female adult prisoners. *Aggressive Behavior, 28*, 257–272.

Lakin, J. L., & Chartrand, T. L. (2005). Excluding and nonconscious behavioral mimicry. In K. D. Williams, J. P. Forgas & W. von Hippel (Eds.), *The social outcast: Ostracism, social exclusion, rejection, and bullying* (pp. 279–295). New York , Hove: Psychology Press.

Lewis, D. (2004). Bullying at work: The impact of shame among university and college lecturers. *British Journal of Guidance & Counselling, 32*, 281–299.

Leymann, H. (1996). The content and development of mobbing at work. *European Journal of Work and Organizational Psychology, 5*, 165–184.

Lind, K., Glasø, L., Pallesen, S., & Einarsen, S. (2009). Personality profiles among targets and nontargets of workplace bullying. *European Psychologist, 14*, 231–237.

Lutgen-Sandvik, P. (2006). Take this job and . . . : Quitting and other forms of resistance to workplace bullying. *Communication Monographs, 73*, 406–433.

Maner, J. K., DeWall, N. C., Baumeister, R. F., & Schaller, M. (2007). Does social exclusion motivate interpersonal reconnection? Resolving the "porcupine problem". *Journal of Personality and Social Psychology, 92*(1), 42–55.

Marchand, A., Demers, A., & Durand, P. (2005). Does work really cause distress? The contribution of occupational structure and work organization to the experience of psychological distress. *Social Science and Medicine*, *61*, 1–14.

Matthiesen, S. B., & Einarsen, S. (2001). MMPI-2 configurations among victims of bullying at work. *European Journal of Work and Organizational Psychology*, *10*, 467–484.

Matthiesen, S. B., & Einarsen, S. (2004). Psychiatric distress and symptoms of PTSD among victims of bullying at work. *British Journal of Guidance and Counselling*, *32*, 335–356.

Monks, C. P., & Coyne, I. (Eds.). (2011). *Bullying in different contexts*. Cambridge: Cambridge University Press.

Nielsen, M., Notelaers, G., & Einarsen, S. (2011). Measuring exposure to workplace bullying. In S. Einarsen, H. Hoel, D. Zapf, & C. L. Cooper (Eds.), *Bullying and harassment in the workplace: Developments in theory, research, and practice*, (pp. 149–176), Boca Raton, London, New York: Taylor & Francis Press.

O'Moore, M., & Kirkham, C. (2001). Self-esteem and its relationship to bullying behavior. *Aggressive Behavior*, *27*, 269–283.

Palmer, E. J., & Thakordas, V. (2005). Relationship between bullying and scores on the Buss-Perry Aggression Questionnaire among imprisoned male offenders. *Aggressive Behavior*, *31*, 56–66.

Pratkanis, A. (2007). Social influence analysis: An index of tactics. In A. Pratkanis (Ed.), *The science of social influence* (pp. 17–82). New York, Hove: Taylor & Francis Group.

Rayner, C. (1997). Bullying at work. *Journal of Community & Applied Social Psychology*, *7*, 177–180.

Salin, D. (2003). Bullying and organisational politics in competitive and rapidly changing work environments. *International Journal of Management and Decision Making*, *4*(1), 35–46.

Smart Richman, L., & Leary, M. R. (2009). Reactions to discrimination, stigmatization, ostracism, and other forms of interpersonal rejection: A multimotive model. *Psychological Review*, *116*, 365–383.

Twenge, J. M. (2005). When does social rejection lead to aggression? The influence of situations, narcissism, emotions, and replenishing connections. In K. D. Williams, J. P. Forgas & W. von Hippel (Eds.), *The social outcast: Ostracism, social exclusion, rejection, and bullying* (pp. 19–34). New York, Hove: Psychology Press.

van Beest, I., & Williams, K. D. (2006). When inclusion costs and ostracism pays, ostracism still hurts. *Journal of Personality and Social Psychology*, *91*, 918–928.

Vartia, M. (1993). The sources of bullying – Psychological work environment and organizational climate. *European Journal of Work and Organizational Psychology*, *5*, 203–214.

Warszewska-Makuch, M. (2007). Polska adaptacja kwestionariusza NAQ do pomiaru mobbingu. *Bezpieczeństwo Pracy*, *12*, 16–19.

Williams, K. D. (2007). Ostracism. *Annual Review of Psychology*, *58*, 425–452.

Williams, K. D., Cheung, C. K. T., & Choi, W. (2000). CyberOstracism: Effects of being ignored over the Internet. *Journal of Personality and Social Psychology*, *79*, 748–762.

Williams, K. D., & Sommer, K. L. (1997). Social ostracism by one's coworkers: Does rejection lead to loafing or compensation? *Personality and Social Psychology Bulletin, 23*, 693–706.

Williams, K. D., & Zadro, L. (2005). Ostracism: The indiscriminate early detection system. In K. D. Williams, J. P. Forgas & W. von Hippel (Eds.), *The social outcast: Ostracism, social exclusion, rejection, and bullying* (pp. 19–34). New York, Hove: Psychology Press.

Zadro, L., Williams, K. D., & Richardson, R. (2004). How low can you go? Ostracism by a computer lowers belonging, control, self-esteem, and meaningful existence. *Journal of Experimental Social Psychology, 40*, 560–567.

Zapf, D., & Gross, C. (2001). Conflict escalation and coping with workplace bullying: A replication and extension. *European Journal of Work and Organizational Psychology, 10*, 497–522.

Bullying the bully: Why zero-tolerance policies get a failing grade

K. Borgwald[1], and H. Theixos[2]
[1]Philosophy Department, Miami Dade College, Miami, FL, USA
[2]Philosophy Department, University of Miami, Coral Gables, FL, USA

Recent studies show that the current punitive approach to bullying, in the form of zero-tolerance policies, is ineffective in reducing bullying and school violence. Despite this significant finding, anti-bullying legislation is increasing. The authors argue that these policies are not only ineffective but that they are also unjust, harmful, and stigmatizing. They advocate a broader integrative approach to bullying programs that includes both victims and bullies.

April 20, 2012 marked the thirteenth anniversary of the Columbine High School shootings. Due in part to the prevailing perception that the Columbine shooters were victims of bullying, schools and the federal government implemented bullying awareness programs with systematic punishments and expulsions. The mechanisms for expulsions are implemented under "zero-tolerance policies," and according to an evidentiary review by the American Psychological Association [APA] (2008), "[zero-tolerance] policies appear to be relatively widespread in America's schools." In order to trigger zero-tolerance policy procedures a student must have committed some sort of bullying/harassment/abuse; the school is then required to expel the student. We say "required" because bullying offenses are not only managed at a local level, but are overseen by multiple federal departments. In short, over the past decade zero-tolerance policies have increased in scope and become more stringent.

In this paper we argue that the recent surge in anti-bullying programs, specifically the prevalence of zero-tolerance policies, has resulted in a counterproductive response to a valid problem. Not only are these policies ineffective in reducing bullying and school violence, and not only are they linked to an increase in covert bullying, we argue that they are also damaging for both the bullies and the bullied. We discuss the stigmatizing social influence of zero-tolerance policies and the "bully label," and we suggest an alternative approach to preventing and responding to bullying behavior, grounded in empathy training.

ZERO-TOLERANCE POLICIES ARE INEFFECTIVE, COUNTERPRODUCTIVE, AND UNJUST

Ineffective

A dominant justification for zero-tolerance policies is that schools cannot tolerate assault. However, research indicates that zero-tolerance policy expulsions are primarily for non-violent offenses, because the definition of bullying includes verbal aggression and other forms of non-physical intimidation. According to national statistics gathered by the Justice Policy Institute and the U.S. Department of Education, crime of all sorts is "down at public schools since 1990—some studies say by as much as 30%. Less than 1% of all violent incidents involving adolescents occur on school grounds" (Finley, 2011, p. 396).

It is tempting to conclude that zero-tolerance policies are causally connected to overall decreases in school violence, but that does not appear to be the case. From the Opposing Viewpoints Series on the prevention of school violence, author Matt Labash (2005, p. 16) notes that:

> One statistical analysis after another shows school violence has been on the decline since 1992—a trend that pre-dates our anti-bullying movement by a good six years... According to the NCES, nearly every indicator of danger in schools is trending downward: from the number of students who claimed they were robbed, to those who got into fights.

Specific studies regarding the efficacy of zero-tolerance suspensions/ expulsions in reducing violence conclude that zero-tolerance policies have had little to no impact on the decline in overall school violence (Skiba, Cohn, & Canter, 2004). Expulsions do not largely respond to school violence (Mendez & Knoff, 2003): over the past decade, 90% of U.S. schools specify that no serious violent crimes were committed in a school year, and that 99% of students do not commit serious crimes while in school (Bear, Cavalier, & Manning, 2002), yet incidences of zero-tolerance expulsions are increasing. It is important to distinguish between incidences of violence in schools (decreasing), incidences of bullying in schools (increasing), and zero-tolerance expulsions (increasing), and to clarify how trends are correlated, but not causally connected.

Because studies show that the majority of school suspensions are not for violent offenses, the question then remains whether school suspensions are the best response to bullying, and this too does not appear to be the case. As reported in a meta-analysis by School Psychology Review (Smith, Schneider, Smith, & Ananiadou, 2004), which reviewed many longitudinal studies, zero-tolerance policies do not show a significant effect on preventing bullying. This meta-analysis reports that the overwhelming majority of whole-school anti-bullying programs (which include zero-tolerance) showed no benefit (86%), or minor benefit (14%), in reducing instances of bullying. In sum, zero-tolerance policies are not causally related to the decline in school violence, nor are they shown to decrease instances of school bullying.

Counterproductive

Zero-tolerance policies are linked to an increase in bullying of a different type. Increasingly, perhaps in response to zero-tolerance policies, bullying is becoming more covert (Woods & Wolke, 2003), and as such zero-tolerance policies are statistically counterproductive in reducing bullying in schools (Evenson, Justinger, Pelischek, & Schulz, 2009; Skiba, 2008). Cyber-bullying and other covert tactics are ways that students continue to bully outside the purvey of zero-tolerance policies. These methods of covert bullying, as well as in-school tactics of shunning, intimidating, ignoring the victim, and other non-physical methods of relational bullying, are not addressed by zero-tolerance policies, as policies aimed at reducing bullying focus on visible cases of bullying, overt bullying, evidenced interpersonally among the students while on campus. Covert and relational bullying are "becoming more prevalent and insidious among students, both as a result of the implementation of improved school policies to deal with overt bullying, and with the advent of new forms of [cyber-bullying]" (Australian Department of Education, Employment, and Workplace Relations, 2009).

In sum, research indicates that zero-tolerance policies are not correlated to the recent decrease in overall school violence, nor do they decrease overall school bullying. Research also indicates that zero-tolerance policies may encourage an adaptation in traditional bullying, to a more covert form of relational bullying. These conclusions alone are enough to argue for a serious revision in anti-bullying methodology.

Unjust

Limiting a child's access to education and treating bullies as criminal offenders can be traced to an influential argument by scholars at Harvard University in 1987: "Under the euphemism of bullying, we see a much broader, more serious affair... Everybody knows these are crimes. The fact that they were committed by minors upon minors does not make them less than crimes."[1] Treating bullying as a crime and removing a child from the school is, in practice, transforming children from being children with behavioral problems into quasi-adults whose rights to an education are forfeited, a form of criminal punishment. If zero-tolerance policies are administered in a legalistic manner (i.e., as a type of state punishment and abridgment of rights), then the implication is that the bully is a type of criminal.

This kind of criminal punishment is unjust on a variety of levels. Data indicates that, in general, school punishments (expulsions, suspensions) are racially disproportionate. Russell Skiba, researcher and professor at Indiana University, has been publishing racial disproportionality studies for two decades (Skiba, Karega Rausch, & Ritter, 2004; Skiba, Michael, Nardo, & Peterson, 2002) and his findings are consistent with studies that show racial disproportionality in school discipline (Wallace, Goodkind, Wallace, & Bachman, 2008). Other biases are also prevalent; for example, students with disabilities make up only about 11% of school populations, but they account for almost 20% of school suspensions (Leone, Malmgren, Mayer, & Meisel, 2000). Discrimination can be attributed equally to the disciplinary philosophy of the school and attitudes of the disciplinarian, as to the specific behavior of the child (Mukuria, 2002), so zero-tolerance punishments are as likely to be discriminatory as are other punishments (Skiba, 2011).

A further injustice occurs because bullies typically come from homes that are physically abusive, lack positive role modeling, and offer inadequate parental attention (Dussich & Maekoya, 2007; Farrington & Hawkins 1991; Kim, Leventhal, Koh, Hubbard, & Boyce, 2006; Roberts & Morotti, 2000). Research indicates that the problematic social behaviors bullies exhibit can be worsened the more time the children spend at home, as research is showing that both victims and bullies are often involved in other forms of victimization within the family and community (National Institute of Mental Health [NIMH], 2012). It is unjust to expel children for exhibiting behaviors they have learned, especially if these behaviors can be unlearned with the right intervention.

Additionally problematic is that expelling bullies significantly increases their likelihood of failing in important developmental markers, and that removing children from their social structure can exacerbate social problems (Mendez, 2003; Santrock, 2004). Bullies who have been expelled from

---

[1] As referenced in Dorothea Ross (2003) Childhood Bullying, Teasing, and Violence: What School Personnel, Other Professionals, and Parents Can Do (Alexandria: American Counseling Association), quoting Greenbaum (1989, p. 11).

schools largely fail to earn a General Equivalency Diploma (GED) or other vocational training compared to their peers, they are more likely to be involved in criminal activity than students who remain in mainstream schools, and have higher rates of depression, drug addiction, home life stresses, and antisocial behavior (Sundius & Farneth, 2008). There are a variety of reasons suspected for these negative outcomes: the original Olweus (1978) study and others have noted that the social community of the bully is especially important to either nurturing or inhibiting adaptive social skills.

In sum, bullies are expelled for a variety of subjective processes which skew against minorities and disabilities, they face a punishment via a quasi-legal process for largely nonviolent and not-illegal acts, and expulsion can exacerbate their problematic behaviors. Part of the punishment is severe abridgment of their access to education; incarcerated juveniles do not lose access to an education, another indication of the discriminatory treatment of bullies. These processes and consequences are unjust to children whose behavior is closely tied to negative experiences in their home-life. One might respond that while this prejudicial treatment is problematic, it is resolvable by the school providing access to an education via off-campus resources. Indeed, expelled children can enroll in home-school programs or other processes in order to obtain a GED, but considering the points made here, separate education is as unjust as expulsion for these non-violent, learned behaviors.

THE SOCIAL INFLUENCE OF ZERO-TOLERANCE POLICIES AND ANTI-BULLYING PROGRAMS

In reviewing anti-bullying literature, specifically studies that analyze the efficacy and impact of zero-tolerance policies, we foresee that a new category of stigmatized other is being created: the bully. In light of how bullying is a complex behavior closely linked to an abusive/chaotic home-life, and that expulsions are often skewed along social biases, we are concerned that bully-labeling further hinders these children from adequately developing pro-social behaviors.

We expect that the bully-label will entrench an experience of otherness and social impairment on the part of the bully, because a common complaint among children is significant anxiety over being perceived as different from other children (Adler & Adler, 1995). Studies exploring the unintended social effects of bully-labeling are sparse, although researchers are sensitive to the potential problem. Those who study the effects of bullying are careful not to increase the stigmatization by labeling certain students as bullies, and also note that for some students bully-labeling is a type of reinforcement of bullying behaviors (Burns, Maycock, Cross, &

Brown, 2008). Awareness on the part of researchers regarding the complex effects of labels is considered a requirement in research methodology, and is an indication of our hypothesis that the social impact of bully-labeling is stigmatizing.

Bullies, for reasons mentioned earlier, are already a kind of victim, and ostracism could exacerbate their social maladjustments. Bullies are children with complex symptomology and psychology, including a prevalence for suicidal ideation (Brunstein Klomek et al., 2008), higher than non-bullies (Brunstein Klomek, Sourander, & Gould, 2011). We do not propose that higher suicidal ideations are due to expulsion and/or bully-labeling, but that the appropriate response to children who bully must seriously consider these factors.

RECOMMENDATIONS: INTEGRATING THE BULLY VIA EMPATHY TRAINING

Inclusion and empathy training: The better approach for the bully

Rather than running the risk of stigmatizing these students, and rather than further supporting an unjust and ineffective system of zero-tolerance, we recommend integrating the bully into the school and the overall social community via whole-school empathy training. To defend this recommendation we appeal to researchers who have identified that a lack of empathy is central to bullying behaviors (Bukowski & Sippola, 1996; Cillessen & Mayeux, 2004; Eisenberg & Mussen, 1989; Estell, Farmer, & Cairns, 2007; Olweus, 1978). Researchers who work on anti-social behavior in children (Berman, 1998; Hoffman, 1979; Kahn & Lawthorne, 2003) strongly believe that social skills and empathy training in schools is vital.

The reasons researchers and educators recommend empathy training in schools are multifaceted. Children who are aggressive, threatening, and/or domineering indicate a lack of appropriate concern for the other, commonly considered a lack of affective empathic concern. Lack of caring-about sentiments are indicated when the child (a) does not recognize and understand the experience of the other, a social cognitive mechanism usually defined as empathy, but also (b) has a difficulty/inability caring about the experience of the other. If lack of empathy is central to the problem of bullying, and empathy can be taught and learned, then empathy training in schools is a better (more just, more inclusive, and likely more beneficial) response to bullying.

Theories that identify empathy as integral to developing pro-social behaviors acknowledge the inborn traits of empathic concern, but emphasize that it can be nurtured through counseling, teaching, and modeling (Eisenberg & Mussen, 1989; Hoffman, 2000; Zhou et al., 2002). A review of literature conducted and published by Kahn and Lawhorne (2003) outlined several school interventions and classroom-based programs designed to teach empathy and reduce bullying behaviors: these models exist; the problem seems to be our general failure to specifically connect them to anti-bullying methodology (with a few exceptions, see Hanish & Guerra, 2000).

Perpetrators accused of wrongdoing experience anxiety due to the threat of rejection from their community (Baumeister, Stillwell, & Heatherton, 1994; Tavuchis, 1991); conversely, a process of inclusion allows perpetrators to experience increased desires to perceive themselves as acceptable people (Baumeister, Stillwell, & Wotman, 1990). Pro-social training has multiple components including interpersonal skill building, clear discussion of acceptable behavior towards others, and constructive ways of managing anger. What the bully needs is to cultivate empathy for the victim, via multiple mechanisms including guilt over their actions (a process Hoffman terms induction; Hoffman 2000).

To assist a bully to change his or her behavior, the bully must be taught how to interact with others, while others are trained in empathizing with bullies. Staub, Pearlman, Gubin, and Hagengimana (2005) found that when perpetrators are shown empathy, their self-image can be repaired; this, in our view, directly pertains to our worry about bully-labeling. Empathy training and inclusion seem to be a step in the right direction of addressing bully-stigmatization, and have been shown to motivate individuals with aggressive social mal-adjustments: perpetrators can be motivated toward pro-social behaviors when their community recognizes their struggles (Nadler & Liviatan, 2004), and has empathy for their emotional distress (McCullough, Wothington, & Rachal, 1997).

Inclusion and empathy training: The better approach for the victim

This process of cultivating empathy is also necessary for victims. We support this claim by drawing on a conception of moral power, and how opportunities to empathize with one's oppressor can be empowering (Card, 2002). Care ethicists, like Nel Noddings (1984), say that we should always strive to be the one who cares, even when our care is rejected or unappreciated. Feminist philosophers have disagreed with Card and Noddings, and worry that encouraging victims to empathize with their oppressors is a type of self-oppression; we recognize this objection, but feel it can be accounted for in an overarching re-conceptualization of the problem of bullying.

Shnabel and Nadler (2008) present a needs-based model of reconciliation, as opposed to conflict resolution, articulating the moral power of victims who cultivate empathy for the perpetrator.[2] The authors point out that much of the literature concerning conflict centers on resolution, usually in the form of agreeing on a redistribution of the resources at stake. Reconciliation, on the other hand, requires the further step of resolving the emotional differences between the conflicting parties. They argue that conflict is accompanied by the opportunity for a social exchange—the opportunity for apology and for forgiveness. Some researchers describe the victim–perpetrator relationship as one of debt (Baumeister et al., 1994), where perpetrators owe victims certain opportunities. These models are ideally situated in an environment where bullies are not expelled but reintegrated into the moral community, and where victims are empowered and guided toward reclaiming their standing in relation to the perpetrator.

With this sort of guidance, both bully and victim can benefit. We are not requiring that the bullied aim to befriend his or her bully, only that an opportunity to repair a relationship be possible. This is a backward-looking notion of empathy tied to causal histories: that our empathy will be weaker for those who have wronged us or our loved ones (Borgwald, 2011). As such the victim is not expected to, or required to forgive the bully, only that schools and society should provide an opportunity for the bully to offer apologies and make amends, and for the victim to attempt understanding. Some researchers emphasize forgiveness (Akhtar, 2002; Minow, 1998; Schönbach, 1990), but we do not claim that forgiveness is the goal, only that expulsion and exclusionary processes inhibit the opportunity for forgiveness, as well as for other repair. Unfortunately the zero-tolerance policy system teaches both the bully and the bullied the power of exclusion and injustice, rather than empathy and concern. According to so many studies cited herein, these policies are worse than simply ineffective: they are likely counterproductive and harmful.

CONCLUSION

Arguments for empathy training in schools and for character-building education are well known in the history of developmental education programs. Empathy training that specifically targets the problem of bullying, however, has been underemphasized in lieu of increased attention and resources toward zero-tolerance legislation (as of this writing, 49 states have additional anti-bullying laws, augmenting federal laws), and we

[2] We begin, in this section, to look at studies that tracked and analyzed perpetrators of abuse and violence, as a means to support our claim for processes that integrate bullies into the moral community. The term "perpetrator" is the term used in these studies. We appropriate the term in order to make a point about bullies who are the perpetrators of harms in schools. We are not completely comfortable with the term as it applies to bullies, but it is accurate when discussing agents of harm, as is "victim" as a term for recipients of harm.

identify this as a central reason for the inefficacy of anti-bullying programs. If we can organize educational strategies that reincorporate the bully into the moral community, and offer a method of empowerment for the bullied, then we theorize (as other educators have, see Lickona, 1991) that this would be the better approach to the problem of bullying, especially when we consider the more covert methods of bullying that zero-tolerance policies do not address. Thus disciplinary policy should shift from an expulsion and punitive model to one that places an emphasis on prevention, empathy, and reintegration. This process addresses overt and covert bullying, aims at incorporating bullies into the social environment rather than relegating them outside it, and empowers victims within a culture of inclusion. Historically schools have struggled to implement this kind of training, but a shift in resources away from exclusionary zero-tolerance programs and toward inclusionary empathy programs should provide the resources schools need.

REFERENCES

Adler, P. A., & Adler, P. (1995). Dynamics of inclusion and exclusion in preadolescent cliques. *Social Psychology Quarterly*, *58*(3), 145–162.

Akhtar, S. (2002). Forgiveness: Origins, dynamics, psychopathology, and technical relevance. *Psychoanalytic Quarterly*, *71*, 175–212.

American Psychological Association Zero-Tolerance Task Force (2008, December). Are zero tolerance policies effective in the schools: An evidentiary review and recommendations. *American Psychologist*, *63*(9), 852–862.

Australian Department of Education, Employment, and Workplace Relations (2009). *Australian Covert Bullying Prevalence Study*. Retrieved July 24, 2012, from: http://www.deewr.gov.au/Schooling/NationalSafeSchools/Documents/covertBullyReports/ACBPS%20chapter%202.pdf

Baumeister, R. F., Stillwell, A. M., & Heatherton, T. F. (1994). Guilt: An interpersonal approach. *Psychological Bulletin*, *115*, 243–267.

Baumeister, R. F., Stillwell, A. M., & Wotman, S. R. (1990). Victim and perpetrator accounts of interpersonal conflict: Autobiographical narratives about anger. *Journal of Personality and Social Psychology*, *59*, 994–1005.

Bear, G. G., Cavalier, A. R., & Manning, M. A. (2002). Best practices in school discipline. In A. Thomas & J. Grimes (Eds.), *Best practices in school psychology IV* (pp. 977–991). Bethesda, MD: National Association of School Psychologists.

Berman, S. H. (1998). The bridge to civility: Empathy, ethics, and service. *School Administrator*, *55*(5), 27–32.

Borgwald, K. E. (2011). Extending care. University of Miami. ProQuest Dissertations and Theses, Retrieved from http://search.proquest.com/docview/871631407?accountid = 14585. (871631407).

Brunstein Klomek, A., Sourander, A., & Gould, M. S. (2011). Bullying and suicide: Detection and intervention. *Psychiatric Times*, *28*(2), 27–28, 30–31.

Brunstein Klomek, A., Sourander, A., Kumpulainen, K., Piha, J., Tamminen, T., Moilanen, I., et al. (2008). Childhood bullying as a risk for later depression and suicidal ideation among Finnish males. *Journal of Affective Disorders*, *109*(1–2), 47–55.

Bukowski, W. M., & Sippola, L. K. (1996). Friendship and morality: (How) are they related? In W. M. Bukowski, A. F. Newcomb, & W. W. Hartup (Eds.), *The company they keep* (pp. 238–261). Cambridge, UK: Cambridge University Press.

Burns, S., Maycock, B., Cross, D., & Brown, G. (2008). The power of peers: Why some students bully others to conform. *Qualitative Health Research*, *18*(12), 1704–1716.

Card, C. (2002). The moral power of victims. In C. Cuomo & A. Bailey (Eds.), *The feminist philosophy reader* (pp. 548–563). New York: McGraw Hill.

Cillessen, A. H. N., & Mayeux, L. (2004). From censure to reinforcement: Developmental changes in the association between aggression and social status. *Child Development*, *75*(1), 147–163.

Dussich, J. P. J., & Maekoya, C. (2007). Physical child harm and bullying-related behaviors: A comparative study in Japan, South Africa, and the United States. *International Journal of Offender Therapy and Comparative Criminology*, *51*(5), 495–509.

Eisenberg, N., & Mussen, P. H. (1989). *The roots of prosocial behavior in children*. Cambridge, UK: Cambridge University Press.

Estell, D. B., Farmer, T. W., & Cairns, B. D. (2007). Bullies and victims in rural African American youth: Behavioral characteristics and social network placement. *Aggressive Behavior*, *33*(2), 145–159.

Evenson, A., Justinger, B., Pelischek, E., & Schulz, S. (2009, Jan/Feb). Zero-tolerance policies and the public schools: When suspension is no longer effective. *NASP Communiqué*, *37*(5). Retrieved September 22, 2012, from: http://www.nasponline.org/publications/cq/mocq375zerotolerance.aspx

Farrington, D. P., & Hawkins, J. D. (1991). Predicting participation, early onset, and later persistence in officially recorded offending. *Criminal Behavior and Mental Health*, *1*, 1–33.

Finley, L. (Ed.). (2011). *Encyclopedia of school crime and violence* (Vol. 1, p. 396). Santa Barbara: ABC-CLIO.

Greenbaum, S. (1989). *Set straight on bullies*. Malibu, CA: National School Safety Center.

Hanish, L. D., & Guerra, N. G. (2000). Children who get victimized at school: What is known? What can be done? *Professional School Counseling*, *4*(2), 113–119.

Hoffman, M. L. (1979). Development of moral thought, feeling, and behavior. *American Psychologist*, *34*(10), 958–966.

Hoffman, M. L. (2000). *Empathy and moral development: Implications for caring and justice*. New York: Cambridge University Press.

Kahn, W. J., & Lawhorne, C. V. (2003). *Empathy: The critical factor in conflict-resolution and a culture of civility*. West Chester PA: University of West Chester. Retrieved April 12, 2012, from EBSCOhost.

Kim, Y. S., Leventhal, B. L., Koh, Y. J., Hubbard, A., & Boyce, W. T. (2006). School bullying and youth violence: Causes or consequences of psychopathologic behavior? *Archives of General Psychiatry*, *63*(9), 10–35.

Labash, M. (2005). Antibullying programs are ineffective and unnecessary. In S. Barbour (Ed.), *How can school violence be prevented?* (pp. 13–23). Farmington Hills, MI: Greenhaven Press.

Leone, P. E., Mayer, M. J., Malmgren, K., & Meisel, S. M. (2000). School violence and disruption: Rhetoric, reality, and reasonable balance. *Focus on Exceptional Children*, *33*(1), 1–20.

Lickona, T. (1991). *Educating for character: How our schools can teach respect and responsibility*. New York: Bantam Books.

McCullough, M. E., Worthington, E. L., & Rachal, K. C. (1997). Interpersonal forgiving in close relationships. *Journal of Personality and Social Psychology*, *73*, 321–336.

Mendez, L. M. (2003). Predictors of suspension and negative school outcomes: A longitudinal investigation. *New Direction Youth Development*, *99*, 17–33.

Mendez, L. M., & Knoff, H. M. (2003). Who gets suspended from school and why: A demographic analysis of schools and disciplinary infractions in a large school district. *Education & Treatment of Children*, *26*, 30–51.

Minow, M. (1998). *Between vengeance and forgiveness: Facing history after genocide and mass violence*. Boston, MA: Beacon Press.

Mukuria, G. (2002). Disciplinary challenges: How do principals address this dilemma? *Urban Education*, *37*(3), 432–452.

Nadler, A., & Liviatan, I. (2004). Intergroup reconciliation process in Israel: Theoretical analysis and empirical findings. In N. R. Branscombe & B. Doosje (Eds.), *Collective guilt: International perspectives* (pp. 216–235). New York: Cambridge University Press.

National Institute of Mental Health (NIMH), Child and Adolescent Violence Research, Publication No. 00-4706, April 2000.

Noddings, N. (1984). *Caring, a feminine approach to ethics & moral education*. Berkeley, CA: University of California Press.

Olweus, D. (1978). *Aggression in the schools: Bullies and whipping boys*. Washington, DC: Hemisphere Publishing.

Roberts Jr, W. J., & Morotti, A. A. (2000). The bully as victim: Understanding bully behaviors to increase the effectiveness of interventions in the bully-victim dyad. *Professional School Counseling*, *4*(2), 148–156.

Ross, D. M. (2003). *Childhood bullying, teasing, and violence: What school personnel, other professionals, and parents can do* (2nd ed.). Alexandria, VA: American Counseling Assn.

Santrock, J. W. (2004). *Life span development* (10th ed.). Boston, MA: McGraw-Hill.

Schönbach, P. (1990). *Account episodes: The management or escalation of conflict*. New York: Cambridge University Press.

Shnabel, N., & Nadler, A. (2008). A needs-based model of reconciliation: Satisfying the differential emotional needs of victim and perpetrator as a key to promoting reconciliation. *Journal of Personality and Social Psychology*, *94*(1), 116–132.

Skiba, R. (2008). Are zero tolerance policies effective in the schools?: An evidentiary review and recommendations. *American Psychologist, 63*(9), 852–862. http://search.ebscohost.com, doi:10.1037/0003-066X.63.9.852.

Skiba, R. J. (2011). Tolrance zro: efficacit et quit. *Cahiers de la scurit: Lcole face au dfi de la securit [Special Issue on School Violence and School Security], 16*, 144–149.

Skiba, R. J., Cohn, A. M., & Canter, A. (2004). Zero tolerance and alternative strategies. In A. S. Canter, L. Z. Paige, M. D. Roth, I. Romero, & S. A. Carroll (Eds.), *Helping children at home and school II: Handouts for family and educators* (Vol. S4, pp. 103–106). Bethesda, MD: National Association of School Psychologists.

Skiba, R., Karega Rausch, M., & Ritter, S. (2004, Summer). Education policy briefs. Children left behind: Series Summary and Recommendations. *Indiana Youth Services Association, 24*(4), (2004). Retrieved November 23, 2008, from: http://www.iub.edu/~safeschl/ChildrenLeftBehind/papers.html

Skiba, R., Michael, R., Nardo, A., & Peterson, R. (2002). The color of discipline: Sources of racial and gender disproportionality in school punishment. *The Urban Review, 34*(4), 317–342.

Smith, J. D., Schneider, B. H., Smith, P. K., & Ananiadou, K. (2004). The effectiveness of whole-school anti-bullying programs: A synthesis of evaluation research. *School Psychology Review, 33*(4), 547–560.

Staub, E., Pearlman, L. A., Gubin, A., & Hagengimana, A. (2005). Healing, reconciliation, forgiving and the prevention of violence after genocide or mass killing: An intervention and its experimental evaluation in Rwanda. *Journal of Social and Clinical Psychology, 24*, 297–334.

Sundias, J., & Farneth, M. (2008). *Putting kids out of school: What's causing suspension rates and why they are detrimental to students, schools, and communities.* Baltimore, MA: Open Society Institute. Retrieved July 21, 2011, from: http://www.soros.org/reports/putting-kids-out-school-whats-causing-high-suspension-rates-and-why-they-are-detrimental

Tavuchis, N. (1991). *Mea culpa: A sociology of apology and reconciliation.* Palo Alto, CA: Stanford University Press.

Wallace, J. M., Goodkind, S., Wallace, C. M., & Bachman, J. G. (2008). Racial, ethnic, and gender differences in school discipline among U. S. high school students: 1991–2005. *The Negro Educational Review, 59*(1–2), 47–62.

Woods, S., & Wolke, D. (2003). Does the content of antibullying policies inform us about the prevalence of direct and relational bullying behaviour in primary schools? *Educational Psychology, 23*, 381–402.

Zhou, Q., Eisenberg, N., Losoya, S. H., Fabes, R. A., Reiser, M., Guthrie, I. K., et al. (2002). The relations of parental warmth and positive expressiveness to children's empathy-related responding and social functioning: A longitudinal study. *Child Development, 73*(3), 893–915.

Friend similarity in attitudes toward bullying and sense of responsibility to intervene

Tiziana Pozzoli and Gianluca Gini
Department of Developmental and Social Psychology, University of Padua, Padua, Italy

This study investigated reciprocal friends' similarity in attitudes toward bullying and responsibility for intervention in favor of the victim among 1485 Italian children (mean age = 10 years, 3 months) and adolescents (mean age = 13 years, 2 months). Findings of two linear regressions confirmed that friend homophily exists in relation to both students' attitudes and responsibility. This result was retained even after individual and friends' bullying and defending behavior were controlled. Similarity between friends emerged particularly when the proportion of reciprocal friends in the classroom was high. Finally, age and gender moderated the relation between individual's and friends' attitudes. These results significantly expand previous findings related to social influences in the bullying phenomenon and have potential interest for researchers and educators.

School bullying is a pervasive problem worldwide, with negative health (Gini & Pozzoli, 2009) and psychosocial (Reijntjes et al., 2011; Ttofi, Farrington, Losel, & Loeber, 2011) consequences. The latest approaches to the study of bullying indicate that the group nature of this phenomenon requires analysis of the role of peer bystanders and how the presence and reactions of this audience can influence the perception of bullies and victims as well as affect students' proneness to adopting specific behaviors (Gini, Pozzoli, Borghi, & Franzoni, 2008; Salmivalli, 2010). In particular, recent bullying research has devoted much effort to understanding why some children personally intervene to stop bullying and help their victimized peers while others support the bullies or simply look the other way (Barchia & Bussey, 2011; Pöyhönen, Juvonen, & Salmivalli, 2010; Pozzoli & Gini, 2010; Sandstrom, Makover, & Bartini, 2012). This focus is important for both theory and intervention, given that a better understanding of which factors enhance or hinder defending behavior within the peer group is one of the core aspects in the development of more effective anti-bullying programs (Porter & Smith-Adcock, 2011; Salmivalli, 2010). In this study we explore how the social context in which students live out their everyday experiences at school—in terms of friend relationships—is related to two important correlates of defending behavior, namely attitudes toward bullying and sense of responsibility for intervention in favor of the victim. More specifically, based on the idea that individual beliefs and moral reactions that lead youngsters to condemn bullying and to support bullied peers can be socialized within meaningful peer relationships, we investigated whether a significant degree of similarity (i.e., homophily) exists between friends with respect to these two characteristics in a large sample of children and adolescents.

Among the factors that may contribute to students' active intervention in favor of a victim, attitudes toward bullying have received great attention. Research has shown a positive association between negative attitudes toward bullying and students' approval of classmates who intervened to stop bullying (Salmivalli & Voeten, 2004). Moreover, anti-bullying attitudes are one of the most important predictors of expressed intention to intervene (Rigby & Slee, 1993) and of actual intervention in favor of victims (Pozzoli & Gini, 2012; Pozzoli, Gini, & Vieno, 2012a; Salmivalli & Voeten, 2004), especially when individuals perceive that similar attitudes are shared among their classmates (Sandstrom et al., 2012). However, attitudes alone do not seem sufficient to explain defending behavior against bullying; actually, other variables are likely to promote the conduct. For example, some authors have stressed the importance of a "moral" assumption of personal responsibility to intervene (Menesini, Codecasa, Benelli, & Cowie, 2003; Menesini, Sanchez, et al., 2003; Pozzoli & Gini, 2010, 2012). Indeed, although students may consider bullying wrong and the victim as not deserving her/his condition, they may do nothing if they think that the responsibility for intervention does not fall to them.

As briefly summarized, both attitudes toward bullying and a sense of responsibility can be considered individual characteristics likely to promote active defending behavior in students who witness bullying situations. However, the study of bullying and its correlates cannot be reduced to the analysis of personal characteristics, especially because this phenomenon involves several processes within the peer group in which bullying takes place (Salmivalli, 2010). In particular, contextual variables in the classroom could influence individual correlates of bystanders' behavior in bullying episodes. The idea that different environments influence individuals is not new. In fact, much has been written on the reciprocal interaction between the individual, family, peers, school, community, and so on (e.g., Bronfenbrenner, 1979; Ladd, 2003; Vieno, Gini, Santinello, Lenzi, & Nation, 2011). Similarly, studies have confirmed that the context in which bullying takes place is likely to influence children's perceptions, attitudes, and behaviors (e.g., Pellegrini & Long, 2002). For example, adherence to peer group norms, social identity concerns, moral climate, and other group mechanisms can contribute to a victim's perceptions and beliefs about bullying (Gini, 2006a, 2008; Nation, Vieno, Perkins, & Santinello, 2008; Nesdale, Milliner, Duffy, & Griffiths, 2009; Pozzoli, Gini, & Vieno, 2012b). These processes of social influence among classmates can be particularly pervasive because school classrooms represent one of the most salient social contexts throughout childhood and adolescence (e.g., Bronfenbrenner, 1979).

As suggested by Prinstein and Dodge (2008), one of the most consistent findings of the social science literature pertains to the remarkably potent effect of peer influence. Groups establish norms and standards of behavior and may pressure members to conform to these norms. The common belief is that students—adolescents above all—exert enormous pressure on one another to behave antisocially. In reality, peer influence is neither always powerful nor always malign. For example, most adolescents are able to resist peer pressure to behave in ways that they consider antisocial, such as stealing (Brown, Lohr, & McClenahan, 1986). Moreover, peer pressure can also be positive. Peers often support and exhort one another to work hard in school, to participate in school activities, or to become involved in community action projects (e.g., Kindermann, 2007).

Some research on peer influence showed that social interactions occur more frequently among similar individuals than among dissimilar individuals. This phenomenon is called "homophily" (Cairns, Cairns, Neckerman, Gest, & Gariépy, 1988). The two explanations commonly proposed for homophily are selection and socialization. Selection effects refer to the tendency of young people to affiliate with peers who exhibit similar attitudes or behaviors to themselves. Several reasons can lead people to establish close relationships with others similar to themselves. For example, Lazer and colleagues (Lazer, Rubineau, Chetkovich, Katz, & Neblo, 2010) have suggested four main motivations for affiliating with others who are similar; it is worth noting that these motivations can also operate outside of conscious awareness: (i) informational: in seeking information, it is better to consult those with apparently similar tastes, beliefs, attitudes; (ii) preferential: others who are similar are more likely to engage in cooperation, while dissimilarity entails greater competition (see the social identity theory, by Tajfel and Turner, 1986); (iii) self-verification: people prefer to interact with others who are likely to understand them as they understand themselves (Swann, Milton, & Polzer, 2000); and (iv) cognitive balance: relationships between individuals who hold dissimilar attitudes are experienced as imbalanced and this imbalance causes discomfort.

Socialization effects, on the other hand, refer to the process by which youths' beliefs and behavior can be affected by their affiliation with other peers, so that similarity between members grows over time as a result of peer influence. Socialization includes both overt forms of influence—for example, actual encouragement from the group to engage in a behavior or to report a certain attitude—or more indirect ones, such as the individuals' tendency to adhere to their perception of group expectations. Starting from this definition, the notion of socialization can be linked to the construct of *conformity*. According to the tripartite model of conformity proposed by Cialdini and Goldstein (2004), individuals are motivated to conform in their behavior, attitudes, or values to fit with group norms depending on the need for accuracy (i.e., the desire to have an accurate perception of the reality in order to respond appropriately to a social situation), affiliation (i.e., the desire to be part of a meaningful social group), and maintenance of a positive self-concept (i.e., the desire to preserve a positive image of oneself).

There is consistent evidence that supports selection and socialization effects to explain a wide variety of behaviors and characteristics, including delinquency, violence, antisocial behavior, risky sexual behavior, and substance use (e.g., Andrews, Tildesley, Hops, & Li, 2002; Dishion, 2000). Interestingly, similar selection and/or socialization effects have been demonstrated for prosocial behaviors and health-promoting behaviors, such as charity work and altruism (e.g., Barry & Wentzel, 2006). Moreover, past research has demonstrated that homophily processes are not limited to the behavioral arena, but they can be extended to attitudes and values, such as homophobic attitudes (Poteat, 2007), hostile attribution tendencies (Halligan & Philips, 2010), and motivational beliefs (Altermatt & Pomerantz, 2003). The main group (i.e., the class group) in which most bullying takes place differs from many social groups in an important aspect: Membership is involuntary and not under individual control, so that the victim cannot easily escape his or her situation and other group members cannot simply leave either. Although students cannot choose their classmates, social selection processes (Kandel, 1978) take place within classrooms, resulting in cliques (that is, highly connected groups of students) and in friendship dyads that consist of similar students. Support for the homophily hypothesis has been documented in the literature on bullying, which has found a relationship between bullying behavior and selection/socialization processes in groups of friends (e.g., Espelage, Holt, & Henkel, 2003; Olthof & Goossens, 2008; Salmivalli, Huttunen, & Lagerspetz, 1997; Witvliet et al., 2010).

However, even though bullying is a group phenomenon and peers are an important source of social learning experiences, previous research on bystanders in bullying has not examined the possibility of peer group homophily in relation to personal correlates of defending behavior, such as students' attitudes toward bullying and sense of personal responsibility for intervention. To fill this gap, in this study we tested the hypothesis that a significant degree of similarity exists between the individual child and his/her friends with respect to these two defending-related constructs. Beyond its theoretical interest, analysis of similarities among friends with respect to characteristics that are potential precursors of actual defending behavior may enhance our understanding of the social mechanisms through which bullying can be tackled.

Based on recent works in different fields (e.g., Halligan & Philips, 2010) that showed that homophily effects are especially strong in reciprocal friendships, we analyzed similarity in attitudes toward bullying and sense of responsibility for intervention between individuals and their reciprocal friends, defined as peers who choose each other (through sociometric nominations) as friends. Moreover, because past research indicated that early adolescents and boys are more susceptible to peer group influence than younger children and girls (although the direction of this influence is sometimes inconsistent across studies; see Brechwald & Prinstein, 2011; Prinstein & Dodge, 2008), we also investigated whether similarity among friends was moderated by age and gender. In this case we expected that similarity between individuals and their friends, in terms of attitudes and sense of responsibility, would be particularly strong in boys and in early adolescents. Finally we hypothesized that the size of the group of reciprocal friends could moderate the association between friends' and individual characteristics. As far as we know, no studies have investigated the potential moderating role of the proportion of reciprocal friends in the classroom on the strength of the homophily effect. Therefore this aim should be considered exploratory.

METHOD

Participants[1]

Of 1644 students invited to participate, 1485 (90.3%) obtained parental consent. Subsequently, 72 students were excluded from the analyses because of lack of reciprocal friends in the classroom. Therefore the final sample consisted of 434 primary school children (48.2% girls; mean age = 10 years,

[1] This study is part of a larger research project on individual and contextual correlates of bystanders' behavior in bullying during childhood and early adolescence (Pozzoli & Gini, 2012; Pozzoli et al., 2012a).

3 month, $SD = 7$ months) and 979 middle school students (47.4% girls; mean age = 13 years, 2 months, $SD = 9$ months). Socio-economic status was not directly measured. However, as in all public schools in Italy, our sample included students from a wide range of social classes (low and working class through upper middle class). In terms of racial/ethnic background, 91.4% of the participants were Italian, 3.4% came from Eastern Europe, 1.7% from Southern Europe, 1.3% from Northern Africa, 0.7% from South America, and the remaining 1.5% from other geographical regions.

Measures

Attitudes toward bullying. Attitudes toward bullying were measured using Salmivalli and Voeten's (2004) scale. Participants were provided with the definition of bullying (see Gini, 2006b) and were asked to evaluate the extent to which they agreed with 10 statements about bullying (e.g., "One should try to help the bullied victims"; "Bullying may be fun sometimes", *reverse coded*) on a 4-point scale (1 = *strongly disagree*, 4 = *strongly agree*). An attitude score against bullying was computed by averaging the students' answers on the 10 items ($\alpha = .76$). The higher a student scored on the scale, the more against bullying his/her attitudes were.

Personal responsibility. Participants' sense of responsibility to intervene in favor of the victim was measured by a 4-item scale (e.g., "Helping classmates who are repeatedly teased, hit or left out is my responsibility"; Pozzoli & Gini, 2010). Participants rated their agreement with each item on a 6-point scale from 1 (totally disagree) to 6 (totally agree). Answers on the four items were averaged to form the personal responsibility score, with higher scores indicating a higher sense of responsibility to intervene ($\alpha = .69$).

Bullying and defending behavior. Bullying others ($\alpha = .82$) and defending the victim ($\alpha = .82$) were measured by means of peer nominations, by asking students to nominate up to three classmates who most often engaged in the behavior described in each item. We used three items for each scale, with one item for each type of bullying: physical (hit or push some classmates), verbal (offend or give nasty nicknames), and relational (exclude some classmates from the group or spread rumors about them) (see Pozzoli & Gini, 2012). These behaviors were measured in order to confirm that any group similarity was not simply an artifact of homophily occurring in relation to behavior.

Friendship nominations. Participants were asked to nominate up to eight of their closest friends (Espelage et al., 2003) in their classroom ($M = 3.9$, $SD = 1.8$, range: 1–8). For each participant the group of reciprocal friends (i.e., peers who were nominated as a friend by the participant and who also nominated him or her) was identified and peer group scores were computed, representing the mean scores of attitudes, responsibility, bullying, and defending behavior of reciprocal friends. Moreover, the proportion of reciprocal friends (PRF; i.e., the number of reciprocal friends divided by the total number of classmates) was calculated for each participant.

RESULTS

Descriptive statistics

Means and standard deviations are presented in Table 1. To test for gender and age differences, a series of *t*-tests were conducted. Effect sizes are expressed as Cohen's *d*. The results showed that girls scored higher than boys in defending behavior and attitudes against bullying. Moreover, girls belonged to groups of friends that scored higher in defending behavior, attitudes against bullying, and sense of responsibility to intervene. In contrast, boys and boys' groups of friends scored higher in bullying behavior. As far as age group is concerned, children scored higher than early adolescents in all of the considered variables, with the exception of proportion of reciprocal friends, for which no difference emerged between the two age groups.

Regression analysis predicting individual attitudes against bullying

We conducted a linear regression analysis to test the hypothesis that friends' attitudes against bullying were related to individual attitudes over and above a set of individual control measures (age-level, gender, PRF, bullying and defending behavior) and friend group control measures (friends' behavior). Moreover, to test for the possible moderating effects of gender, age and PRF on the association between friends' and individual attitudes, the two-way interaction terms were entered. None of the three- or four-way interactions was significant and they were excluded from analysis.

The model explained 20% of the variance in individual attitudes against bullying. As far as control variables are concerned, younger age ($\beta = -.12$, $t = -4.60$, $p < .001$), being a girl ($\beta = .06$, $t = 2.04$, $p = .04$), lower levels of bullying ($\beta = -.15$, $t = -5.57$, $p < .001$), higher levels of defending behavior ($\beta = .11$, $t = 3.87$, $p < .001$), and lower levels of bullying by reciprocal friends ($\beta = -.06$, $t = -1.95$, $p = .05$) predicted attitudes against bullying. After controlling for these variables, friends' attitudes ($\beta = .22$, $t = 3.92$, $p < .001$) significantly predicted individual attitudes. Moreover, all of the two-way interactions were significant (friends' attitudes × gender: $\beta = -.08$, $t = -2.48$, $p = .01$; friends' attitudes × age group: $\beta = .13$, $t = 2.60$, $p = .01$; friends' attitudes × PRF: $\beta = .10$, $t = 3.83$, $p < .001$). Results derived from

TABLE 1
Descriptive statistics and comparisons by Gender and Age Group

	Full sample *(N = 1413)* *Mean (SD)*	*Boys* *(N = 740)* *Mean (SD)*	*Girls* *(N = 673)* *Mean (SD)*	*t-test* *(gender)*	*d*	*Children* *(N = 434)* *Mean (SD)*	*Early adolescents* *(N = 979)* *Mean (SD)*	*t-test* *(age group)*	*d*
Proportion of reciprocal friends	.23 (.12)	.23 (.12)	.23 (.12)	.03	.00	.23 (.13)	.23 (.12)	.52	.00
Bullying	.27 (.41)	.41 (.51)	.13 (.19)	13.46***	.72	.35 (.48)	.23 (.37)	4.91***	.28
Defending	.29 (.31)	.21 (.22)	.38 (.36)	–10.47***	.57	.36 (.34)	.26 (.29)	5.29***	.32
Attitudes toward bullying	3.47 (.44)	3.38 (.47)	3.56 (.38)	–8.01***	.42	3.57 (.38)	3.42 (.45)	5.92***	.36
Personal responsibility	3.90 (.1.02)	3.85 (1.05)	3.95 (.98)	–1.90	.10	4.00 (1.01)	3.85 (1.02)	2.50*	.15
Friends' bullying	.25 (.25)	.34 (.28)	.16 (.16)	14.84***	.79	.32 (.28)	.22 (.22)	6.74***	.40
Friends' defending	.32 (.21)	.27 (.17)	.38 (.14)	–10.54***	.71	.39 (.23)	.29 (.19)	8.62***	.47
Friends' attitudes toward bullying	3.47 (.30)	3.40 (.31)	3.54 (.27)	–8.59***	.48	3.56 (.26)	3.43 (.31)	7.77***	.45
Friends' responsibility	3.91 (.65)	3.86 (.67)	3.97 (.63)	–3.18**	.17	4.01 (.65)	3.87 (.65)	3.64***	.21

$^{*}p < .05$, $^{**}p < .01$, $^{***}p < .001$.

simple slope computations revealed that friends' levels of attitudes against bullying were more strongly related to different levels of individual attitudes among boys (b = .33, SE = .08, t = 3.90, p < .001) than among girls (b = .15, SE = .08, t = 1.88, p = .06). Moreover, the positive relation between friends and individual attitudes was stronger among early adolescents (b = .55, SE = .04, t = 12.21, p < .001) than among children (b = .33, SE = .08, t = 3.90, p < .001); the same was true when PRF was high (+1 SD; b = .46, SE = .10, t = 4.71, p < .001) as opposed to low (−1 SD) PRF (b = .20, SE = .08, t = 2.35, p = .02).

Regression analysis predicting individual responsibility for intervention

The same procedure was used to analyze the association between friends' and individual sense of responsibility to intervene. Individual responsibility was negatively associated with bullying (β = −.07, t = −2.26, p = .02) and positively associated with defending behavior (β = .13, t = 4.30, p < .001). As hypothesized, friends' sense of responsibility positively predicted individual sense of responsibility to intervene in bullying episodes (β = .14, t = 2.48, p = .01). Interestingly, this effect was moderated by PRF (β = .08, t = 2.99, p = .003), in that it was significant only when the PRF was high (+1 SD; b = .34, SE = .10, t = 3.28, p = .001). In contrast, when the PRF was low (−1 SD) there was no association between friends' and individual sense of responsibility (b = .08, SE = .08, t = .99, p = .32). The model explained 6% of the variance in individual sense of responsibility to intervene.

Finally, given that some children were reciprocal friends of more than one classmate, in order to control for the possibility that a certain degree of redundancy in the data might affect the results of the regression analyses, we recompleted analyses with a reduced randomly selected data set in which every case was counted only once (Halligan & Philips, 2010). The results of these analyses confirmed our original results in terms of explained variance and direction of effects.

DISCUSSION

The key finding of the present study was the observation of a significant association between students' attitudes and sense of responsibility and those of their friends in a large sample of children and early adolescents. Importantly, this association was retained even once individuals' and friends' levels of bullying and defending behavior were controlled for. This is the first study that has demonstrated that friend homophily exists in relation to these two defending-related variables, even though at this time we cannot draw any conclusion about the relative contributions of socialization and/or selective affiliation processes to the observed group homophily. Indeed, both processes are likely to occur, and longitudinal studies are required in order to identify the unique contribution of each of these two processes. Moreover, it might be possible that similarity in attitudes and sense of responsibility is secondary to homophily in bullying or defending behavior. However, the fact that associations between individuals and their friends were retained when individual and friend group levels of bullying and defending were controlled for provides evidence against this interpretation.

The analysis of attitudes toward bullying confirmed the moderating role of gender and age, so that homophily with respect to attitudes was stronger among boys and older participants (Prinstein & Dodge, 2008). As far as age differences are concerned, this result is consistent with past research that has underlined the growing importance of peers in influencing beliefs, attitudes, and norms during the middle school years (Bukowski, Newcomb, & Hartup, 1996; Harris, 1995; Juvoven & Galvàn, 2008; Pozzoli et al., 2012a). On the other hand, gender differences are particularly interesting. Indeed, most research has suggested that boys are more influenced by peers than girls are, especially in terms of peer pressure toward misbehavior (Prinstein & Dodge, 2008; Sim & Koh, 2003). In the present study the greater tendency of boys to conform to friends' attitudes against bullying extends the previous results to another domain, one that is positive. Obviously this result must be considered as preliminary and further research is needed to better understand the process of influence underlying this finding.

As regards individuals' and friends' sense of responsibility to intervene, age and gender did not affect the association between these two variables. This is not totally surprising because, as suggested by Brechwald and Prinstein (2011), influence processes among peers may be different based on the investigated variables. Further studies are needed to better explore this issue. For example, it could be interesting to analyze how individual gender and age are associated with different levels of similarity within a group, depending on the friends' genders and ages.

Another remarkable result concerns the moderating role played by the proportion of reciprocal friends, so that similarity between friends emerged in particular when PRF is high. In past studies the characteristics of the group of friends have been under-studied, although it is fully recognized that features of the friendship group can be important moderators of the group influence effects (Brechwald & Prinstein, 2011). For example, Ellis and Zarbatany (2007) found that groups with greater centrality—which can be considered as a characteristic related to the visibility of the group—were more potent sources of influence with respect to several behaviors (e.g., prosocial behavior, relational aggression). Similarly, with regard to moderation by PRF, we may hypothesize that being part of a friend group composed of a proportionally large number of classmates can lead a student to consider that thoughts and beliefs conveyed by friends could be more accepted by students in the classroom. So agreeing with or adapting to these opinions could be convenient, considering that this will likely lead to peer acceptance.

This result is also consistent with some theories in the social psychology domain. For example, in light of the aforementioned tripartite model of conformity (Cialdini & Goldstein, 2004), it is likely that when a student's attitudes are similar to those of a consistent number of classmates, he/she will be more inclined to consider those attitudes as appropriate (need for accuracy) and to believe that he/she will be accepted and appreciated if he/she should express them (need for maintenance of a positive self-concept). Moreover, belonging to a large group—likely to be more influential in the class than a small group—satisfies the need for being part of a meaningful social group, that is, the third motivation suggested by Cialdini and Goldstein (2004) for explaining conformity within groups. Another example derives from one of the central postulates of the dynamic social impact theory developed by Latané (1996); that is, that an individual is more likely to conform to the attitudes, beliefs, values, and behavior exhibited by the "local numerical majority" (i.e., the majority in a specific context) than by either the minority or by less-proximate people.

The results on the role of PRF also raise questions about the nature of the majority view in bullying. In fact, although the relationship between number of people and social influence has been demonstrated in different settings (e.g., embarrassment, bystander intervention, productivity in groups; Latané & Wolf, 1981; Novak, Szamrej, & Latané, 1990), we may ask whether the belief is as readily transmittable if it is pro- or anti-bullying. Addressing these issues will provide an important direction for future research.[2]

In sum, the results of this study may be regarded as an example of how social influences in the classroom—in the form of friends' attitudes toward bullying and sense of responsibility to intervene—might help to explain students' beliefs and moral values related to the bullying phenomenon during late childhood and early adolescence. Moreover, these findings stress the importance of also considering contextual influences on these characteristics, which might be considered as merely individual.

Some limitations must be acknowledged. First, as mentioned above, the cross-sectional nature of the study did not allow us to arrive at any conclusions about specific mechanisms underlying the similarity between individuals and their friends. To this end, longitudinal studies are required. In addition, longitudinal research would allow us to understand the relationship between attitudinal homophily and behavioral homophily, as well as to clarify whether one of them emerges from the other or whether they are two independent mechanisms. Moreover, longitudinal designs would allow us to investigate whether and how homophily among friends

[2] We thank an anonymous reviewer for this suggestion.

changes with development, and whether it could be extended to younger and older students than those considered in our study.

Moreover, we focused on few aspects of peer groups; that is, the friendship reciprocity of its members and the size of the group. However, it is plausible that other characteristics of the friend group could enhance or decrease similarity among its members. For example, it would be interesting to investigate the role played by gender composition, by friends' status in the classroom, or by the duration and quality of the relationships among friends, for example, in terms of reciprocal support or sharing values and expectations. Linked to this last point, in this study we focused on similarity in self-reported attitudes and responsibility, while we did not explore individual perception of friends' attitudes and responsibility. Future research should analyze whether homophily among friends might be moderated by a more or less accurate individual perception of friends' characteristics. In other words, it would be fascinating to investigate whether pluralistic ignorance—that is, the discrepancy between actual and perceived group characteristics (Sandstrom et al., 2012)—can affect the individual tendency to conform to friends' attitudes and values.

Finally, the amount of variance in sense of responsibility to intervene as explained by our model was substantially smaller than the variance accounted for by the same variables with respect to attitudes against bullying. The different nature of the two variables can play a role in explaining this difference. Personal responsibility for intervention—that is, a moral assumption of personal responsibility to intervene—can be deemed as a more intra-individual variable. Conversely, attitudes can be considered a more "explicit" characteristic; indeed, attitudes refer to people's opinions and beliefs on bullying and to the way they deal with this kind of aggressive behavior. People can easily talk about or confront one another on their attitudes towards bullying, but this is more difficult when the subject of discussion is the personal responsibility for intervention. In other words, we think that the sense of responsibility is less easily socialized or shared among peers than attitudes are. As a consequence, it is more difficult to conform to something that is not clear. This could explain the smaller amount of variance explained by friend group variables.

Despite these limitations this study adds some important knowledge to the so-far limited literature about influences among peers with respect to variables related to bystander participation in bullying, clearly documenting the need for a social-ecological approach to the study of bullying correlates. Moreover the current results, albeit preliminary, may have implications for anti-bullying interventions. First, they confirm the significant role of the peer group in bullying and suggest that, consistent with a more ecologically valid approach to the phenomenon, anti-bullying interventions should address the individuals involved as well as their peer group (Espelage &

Swearer, 2004). For example, they suggest that we should be more aware of the friendship networks within the classroom and of how these close relationships may impact on desired outcomes, such as correlates of active defending behavior. In this respect, interventions should include activities in social processes, such as identification and modeling processes within the friend group, and development and sharing of positive group norms. Moreover, assertiveness training may be especially useful as an intervention, given that it can help students to resist negative friend pressure and adopt behavior consistent with their own attitudes or moral values, even when this is not what other pupils in their group expect or are perceived as expecting.

REFERENCES

Altermatt, E. R., & Pomerantz, E. M. (2003). The development of competence-related and motivational beliefs: An investigation of similarity and influence among friends. *Journal of Educational Psychology*, *95*, 111–123. doi: 10.1037/0022-0663.95.1.111.

Andrews, J. A., Tildesley, E., Hops, H., & Li, F. (2002). The influence of peers on young adult substance use. *Health Psychology*, *21*, 349–357. doi: 10.1037/0278-6133.21.4.349.

Barchia, K., & Bussey, K. (2011). Predictors of student defenders of peer aggression victims: Empathy and social cognitive factors. *International Journal of Behavioral Development*, *35*, 1–9. doi: 10.1177/0165025410396746.

Barry, C. M., & Wentzel, K. R. (2006). Friend influence on prosocial behavior: The role of motivational factors and friendship characteristics. *Developmental Psychology*, *42*, 153–163. doi: 10.1037/0012-1649.42.1.153.

Brechwald, W. A., & Prinstein, M. J. (2011). Beyond homophily: A decade of advances in understanding peer influence processes. *Journal of Research on Adolescence*, *21*, 166–179. doi: 10.1111/j.1532-7795.2010.00721.x.

Bronfenbrenner, U. (1979). *The ecology of human development: Experiments by nature and design*. Cambridge, MA: Harvard University Press.

Brown, B. B., Lohr, M. J., & McClenahan, E. L. (1986). Early adolescents' perceptions of peer pressure. *Journal of Early Adolescence*, *6*, 139–154. doi: 10.1177/0272431686062005.

Bukowski, W. M., Newcomb, A. F., & Hartup, W. W. (1996). *The company they keep: Friendship in childhood and adolescence*. New York: Cambridge University Press.

Cairns, R. B., Cairns, B. D., Neckerman, H. J., Gest, S., & Gariépy, J. L. (1988). Social networks and aggressive behavior: Peer support or peer rejection? *Developmental Psychology*, *24*, 815–823. doi: 10.1037/0012-1649.24.6.815.

Cialdini, R. J., & Goldstein, N. J. (2004). Social influence: Compliance and conformity. *Annual Review of Psychology*, *55*, 591–621. doi: 10.1146/annurev.psych.55.090902.142015.

Dishion, T. (2000). Cross-setting consistency in early adolescent psychopathology: Deviant friendships and problem behavior sequelae. *Journal of Personality*, *68*, 1109–1126. doi: 10.1111/1467-6494.00128.

Ellis, W. E., & Zarbatany, L. (2007). Peer group status as a moderator of group influence on children's deviant, aggressive, and prosocial behavior. *Child Development*, *78*, 1240–1254. doi: 10.1111/j.1467-8624.2007.01063.x.

Espelage, D., Holt, M., & Henkel, R. (2003). Examination of peer-group contextual effects on aggression during early adolescence. *Child Development*, *74*, 205–220. doi: 10.1111/1467-8624.00531.

Espelage, D. L., & Swearer, S. M. (2004). *Bullying in American schools: A social-ecological perspective on prevention and intervention*. Mahweh, NJ: Lawrence Erlbaum Associates Inc.

Gini, G. (2006a). Bullying as a social process: The role of group membership in students' perception of inter-group aggression at school. *Journal of School Psychology*, *44*, 51–65. doi:10.1016/j.jsp.2005.12.002.

Gini, G. (2006b). Social cognition and moral cognition in bullying: What's wrong? *Aggressive Behavior*, *32*(6), 528–539. doi: 10.1002/ab.20153.

Gini, G. (2008). Italian elementary and middle school students blaming the victim of bullying and perception of school moral atmosphere. *Elementary School Journal*, *108*, 1–20. doi:10.1086/528975.

Gini, G., & Pozzoli, T. (2009). Association between bullying and psychosomatic problems: A Meta-analysis. *Pediatrics*, *123*, 1059–1065. doi:10.1542/peds.2008-1215.

Gini, G., Pozzoli, T., Borghi, F., & Franzoni, L. (2008). The role of bystanders in students' perception of bullying and sense of safety. *Journal of School Psychology*, *46*, 617–638. doi:10.1016/j.jsp.2008.02.001.

Halligan, S. L., & Philips, K. J. (2010). Are you thinking what I'm thinking? Peer group similarities in adolescent hostile attribution tendencies. *Developmental Psychology*, *46*, 1385–1388. doi: 10.1037/a0020383.

Harris, J. R. (1995). Where is the child's environment? A group socialization theory of development. *Psychological Review*, *102*, 458–489. doi: 10.1037/0033-295X.102.3.458.

Juvonen, J., & Galvan, A. (2008). Peer influence in involuntary social groups: Lessons from research on bullying. In M. Prinstein & K. Dodge (Eds.), *Peer influence processes among youth* (pp. 225–244). New York: Guilford Press.

Kandel, D. B. (1978). Homophily, selection, and socialization in adolescent friendships. *American Journal of Sociology*, *84*, 427–436. doi: 10.1086/226792.

Kindermann, T. A. (2007). Effects of naturally-existing peer groups on changes in academic engagement in a cohort of sixth graders. *Child Development*, *78*, 1186–1203. doi: 10.1111/j.1467-8624.2007.01060.x.

Ladd, G. W. (2003). Probing the adaptive significance of children's behavior and relationships in the school context: A child-by-environment perspective. In R. Kail (Ed.), *Advances in child behavior and development* (pp. 43–104). New York: Wiley.

Latané, B. (1996). Dynamic social impact: The creation of culture by communication. *Journal of Communication*, *4*, 13–25. doi: 10.1111/j.1460-2466.1996.tb01501.x.

Latané, B., & Wolf, S. (1981). The social impact of majorities and minorities. *Psychological Review*, *88*, 438–453. doi: 10.1037/0033-295X.88.5.438.

Lazer, D., Rubineau, B., Katz, N., Chetkovich, C., & Neblo, M. (2010). The co-evolution of networks and political attitudes. *Political Communication*, *27*, 248–274. doi: 10.1080/10584609.2010.500187.

Menesini, E., Codecasa, E., Benelli, B., & Cowie, H. (2003). Enhancing children's responsibility to take action against bullying: Evaluation of a befriending intervention in Italian middle schools. *Aggressive Behavior*, *29*, 1–14. doi: 10.1002/ab.80012.

Menesini, E., Sanchez, V., Fonzi, A., Ortega, R., Costabile, A., & Lo Feudo, G. (2003). Moral emotions and bullying: A cross-national comparison of differences between bullies, victims and outsiders. *Aggressive Behavior*, *29*, 515–530. doi: 10.1002/ab.10060.

Nation, M., Vieno, A., Perkins, D. D., & Santinello, M. (2008). Bullying in school and adolescent sense of empowerment: An analysis of relationships with parents, friends, and teachers. *Journal of Community and Applied Social Psychology*, *18*, 211–232. doi: 10.1002/casp.921.

Nesdale, D., Milliner, E., Duffy, A., & Griffiths, J. A. (2009). Group membership, group norms, empathy, and young children's intentions to aggress. *Aggressive Behavior*, *35*, 244–258. doi: 10.1002/ab.20303.

Nowak, M. A., Szamrej, J., & Latané, B. (1990). From private attitude to public opinion: A dynamical theory of social impact. *Psychological Review*, *97*, 362–376. doi: 10.1037//0033-295X.97.3.362.

Olthof, T., & Goossens, F. (2008). Bullying and the need to belong: Early adolescents' bullying-related behavior and the acceptance they desire and receive from particular classmates. *Social Development*, *17*, 24–46. doi: 10.1111/j.1467-9507.2007.00413.x.

Pellegrini, A. D., & Long, J. D. (2002). A longitudinal study of bullying, dominance, and victimization during the transition from primary school through secondary school. *British Journal of Developmental Psychology*, *20*, 259–280. doi: 10.1348/026151002166442.

Porter, J. R., & Smith-Adcock, S. (2011). Children who help the victims of bullying: Implications for practice. *International Journal of the Advancement of Counselling*, *33*, 196–205. doi: 10.1007/s10447-011-9121-9.

Poteat, V. P. (2007). Peer group socialization of homophobic attitudes and behavior during adolescence. *Child Development*, *78*, 1830–1842. doi: 10.1111/j.1467-8624.2007.01101.x.

Pöyhönen, V., Juvonen, J., & Salmivalli, C. (2010). What does it take to defend the victimized peer? The interplay between personal and social factors. *Merrill-Palmer Quarterly*, *56*, 143–163. doi: 10.1353/mpq.0.0046.

Pozzoli, T., & Gini, G. (2010). Active defending and passive bystanding behavior in bullying: The role of personal characteristics and perceived peer pressure. *Journal of Abnormal Child Psychology*, *38*(6), 815–827. doi: 10.1007/s10802-010-9399-9.

Pozzoli, T., & Gini, G. (2012). Why do bystanders of bullying help or not? A multidimensional model. *Journal of Early Adolescence*. Advance online publication. doi: 10.1177/0272431612440172.

Pozzoli, T., Gini, G., & Vieno, A. (2012a). The role of individual correlates and class norms in defending and passive bystanding behavior in bullying: A multilevel analysis. *Child Development*. Advance online publication. doi: 10.1111/j.1467-8624.2012.01831.x.

Pozzoli, T., Gini, G., & Vieno, A. (2012b). Individual and class moral disengagement in bullying among elementary school children. *Aggressive Behavior*, *38*, 378–388. doi:10.1002/ab.21442.

Prinstein, M. J., & Dodge, K. A. (2008). *Understanding peer influence in children and adolescents*. New York: Guilford Press.

Reijntjes, A., Kamphuis, J. H., Prinzie, P., Boelen, P. A., van der Schoot, M., & Telch, M. J. (2011). Prospective linkages between peer victimization and externalizing problems in children: A meta-analysis. *Aggressive Behavior*, *37*, 215–222. doi: 10.1002/ab.20374.

Rigby, K., & Slee, P. T. (1993). Dimensions of interpersonal relation among Australian children and implications for psychological well-being. *Journal of Social Psychology*, *133*, 33–42.

Salmivalli, C. (2010). Bullying and the peer group: A review. *Aggression and Violent Behavior*, *15*, 112–120. doi: 10.1016/j.avb.2009.08.007.

Salmivalli, C., Huttunen, A., & Lagerspetz, K. (1997). Peer networks and bullying in schools. *Scandinavian Journal of Psychology*, *38*, 305–312. doi: 10.1111/1467-9450.00040.

Salmivalli, C., & Voeten, M. (2004). Connections between attitudes, group norms, and behaviour in bullying situations. *International Journal of Behavioral Development*, *28*, 246–258. doi: 10.1080/01650250344000488.

Sandstrom, M., Makover, H., & Bartini, M. (2012). Social context of bullying: Do misperceptions of group norms influence children's responses to witnessed episodes? *Social Influence*. Advance online publication. doi: 10.1080/15534510.2011.651302.

Sim, T. N., & Koh, S. F. (2003). A domain conceptualization of adolescent susceptibility to peer pressure. *Journal of Research on Adolescence*, *13*, 5–80. doi: 10.1111/1532-7795.1301002.

Swann, W. B., Milton, L. P., & Polzer, J. T. (2000). Should we create a niche or fall in line? Identity negotiation and small group effectiveness. *Journal of Personality and Social Psychology*, *79*, 238–250. doi: 10.1037//0022-3514.79.2.238.

Tajfel, H., & Turner, J. C. (1986). The social identity theory of inter-group behavior. In S. Worchel & L. W. Austin (Eds.), *Psychology of intergroup relations* (pp. 7–24). Chicago: Nelson-Hall.

Ttofi, M. M., Farrington, D. P., Losel, F., & Loeber, R. (2011). The predictive efficiency of school bullying versus later offending: A systematic/meta-analytic review of longitudinal studies. *Criminal Behavior and Mental Health*, *21*, 80–89. doi: 10.1002/cbm.808.

Vieno, A., Gini, G., Santinello, M., Lenzi, M., & Nation, M. (2011). Violent behavior and unfairness in school: Multilevel analysis of Italian schools. *Journal of Community Psychology*, *39*, 534–550. doi: 10.1002/jcop.20450.

Witvliet, M., Olthof, T., Hoeksma, J., Smits, M., Koot, H., & Goossens, F. (2010). Peer group affiliation of children: The role of perceived popularity, likeability, and behavioral similarity in bullying. *Social Development*, *19*, 285–303. doi: 10.1111/j.1467-9507.2009.00544.x.

Overt and relational victimization and adolescent friendships: Selection, de-selection, and social influence

Jelle J. Sijtsema[1,2,3], Ashwin J. Rambaran[4], and Tiina J. Ojanen[5]
[1]Interuniversity Center for Social Science Theory and Methodology, University of Groningen, Groningen, the Netherlands
[2]Interdisciplinary Center Psychopathology and Emotion Regulation, University of Groningen, University Medical Center Groningen, Groningen, the Netherlands
[3]Developmental Psychology, Tilburg University, Tilburg, the Netherlands
[4]Department of Sociology, University of Groningen, Groningen, the Netherlands
[5]Department of Psychology, University of South Florida, Tampa, FL, USA

This study examined friendship selection and social influence in overt and relational victimization during middle school ($N = 504$; 12–14 years) using longitudinal social network analysis. Relational victimization was related to undesirability as a friend (i.e., receiving fewer friendship nominations from peers) and to selecting friends who experienced similar levels of relational victimization. Overt victimization was related to being less active in nominating peers as friends and showed maintenance of friendship ties in one friendship network, but termination or de-selection of friendships in another. Social influence was observed for both forms of victimization. The findings provide evidence for both friendship selection and social influence in victimization, suggest that victimized youth may have friendship difficulties, and underline the need to consider overt and relational victimization separately to understand the development of victimization.

Victimization by peers constitutes one of the most prominent problems in adolescence: it increases internalizing difficulties (Reijntjes, Kamphuis, Prinzie, & Telch, 2010) and compromises the development of healthy peer relationships (Crick et al., 2001; Sainio, Veenstra, Huitsing, & Salmivalli, 2011; Salmivalli & Peets, 2009). Although increasingly studied, there are several gaps in the current literature. First, little is known about victimization in terms of friendship selection and social influence. Second, previous studies have largely neglected the distinction between overt victimization involving direct physical or verbal attacks, and relational victimization involving social manipulation (e.g., rumor spreading) that deprives youth from opportunities to gain closeness, acceptance, and friendship (Crick, Casas, & Nelson, 2002). However, research on these specific forms of victimization is especially important in adolescence where victimization is increasingly relational in nature (Heilbron & Prinstein, 2008). To advance our understanding of the social developmental processes in victimization, we aimed to overcome these gaps by studying overt and relational victimization in association with friendship selection, de-selection, and social influence processes during adolescence.

VICTIMIZATION: FRIENDSHIP SELECTION, DE-SELECTION, AND SOCIAL INFLUENCE

Friendships are critical for adolescents as they provide support, affection, and behavioral confirmation (Newcomb & Bagwell, 1995). The need for affective relationships is universal (Lindenberg, 1996; Pendell, 2002) and becomes increasingly important during adolescence (Marsh, Allen, Ho, Porter, & McFarland, 2006). Friendships tend to involve homophily or similarity between friends (Kandel, 1978; McPherson, Smith-Lovin, & Cook, 2001), which may be driven by social selection, influence, or both (Steglich, Snijders, & Pearson, 2010; Veenstra & Dijkstra, 2011). That is, youth similar in psychological or behavioral characteristics are likely to select each other as friends (selection-similarity) and may also grow more similar to each other over time (social influence). To reliably examine either process, both need to be simultaneously assessed to control for their potential inter-dependencies in longitudinal data (Snijders, van de Bunt, & Steglich, 2010).

Victimized youth face several challenges when it comes to friendships. They are often rejected by peers (Hodges, Malone, & Perry, 1997), have fewer friends than bullies and other children (Eslea et al., 2004), and are less likely to be nominated as friends (Mouttapa, Valente, Gallaher, Rohrbach, & Unger, 2004). Victimization is also related to poor social skills (Fox & Boulton, 2006), which may compromise the ability to establish and maintain friendships. Youth with victimized friends are also often rejected by peers (Ray, Cohen, Secrist, & Duncan, 1997), suggesting that the marginalized status of victimized youth may reflect upon their friends who may also become rejected or victimized over time.

The above suggests that victimized youth are unattractive as friends and may settle for the second best in friendships. This process, known as default selection (Deptula & Cohen, 2004; Sijtsema, Lindenberg, & Veenstra, 2010), implies that one may want, but is not able, to befriend prosocial or popular peers. Instead victimized youth may settle for friendships with equally victimized peers (selection-similarity) to gain affection, or potentially to co-ruminate over shared negative experiences. Research on friendships of rejected (Deptula & Cohen, 2004) and aggressive youth (Sijtsema, Lindenberg, et al., 2010) supports the default selection hypothesis.

However, friendships with overtly as well as relationally victimized peers involve conflicts (Bagwell & Schmidt, 2011) and victimized friends provide fewer benefits than non-victimized friends (Fox & Boulton, 2006). Therefore, although youth may initially select friends similar in victimization, these relationships may be broken off relatively easily across time. Such de-selection processes in social development are still little understood at this time (Veenstra & Dijkstra, 2011), but may apply to friendships of victimized youth as they provide fewer benefits than friendships among non-victimized youth and involve co-rumination of shared negative experiences similarly to rejected youth with emotional difficulties (Rose, Carlson, & Waller, 2007). Moreover, affiliating with victimized friends may increase the risk of being rejected and victimized over time (Ray et al., 1997). Based on this literature we tested two hypotheses with regard to friendship selection in this study: a *selection similarity hypothesis* stating that similarity in victimization predicts similarity friendship selection, and a *de-selection hypothesis* stating that similarity in victimization also predicts friendship de-selection or termination of friendships over time.

Similarity between friends may also result from social influence. This means that youth become more similar to their friends in terms of behaviors or attitudes and this can be facilitated by increasingly sharing attention and positive responses to particular experiences (Dishion, Piehler, & Myers, 2008). For example, victimized youth may co-ruminate over experiences of victimization which may mutually intensify emotional difficulties (Rose et al., 2007), thus leading to higher tendencies to report more victimization. Alternatively, friends of victimized youth may witness a decrease in social status due to affiliating with victimized peers and hence become increasingly victimized themselves over time (Ray et al., 1997). Thus social influence in victimization may be facilitated by both psychological and social processes in the peer group. It is important to note that social influence may facilitate either increasing or decreasing levels of victimization. That is, next to the previously described negative social influence effects, friendships may also shield against victimization (Wang, Iannotti, & Nansel, 2009), emotional difficulties (Hodges, Boivin, Vitaro & Bukowski, 1999), and negative self-perception (Adams, Santo, & Bukowski, 2011). In the context of victimization it is thus important to examine whether victimized youth who have non-victimized friends also decrease in victimization over time. In short, regardless of the direction of influence, our *social influence hypothesis* proposed that longitudinal change in victimization depends on friends' level of victimization.

CONSIDERING THE FORM OF VICTIMIZATION

Because overt and relational victimization operate differently in friendships it is important to study friendship selection and influence separately for each form. Unlike overt victimization, relational victimization often occurs within friendships, involving threats of affection loss or damaged relationships (Crick & Nelson, 2002). Thus relationally victimized youth may fear establishing friendships with peers dissimilar in relational victimization for uncertainty of the outcome, and befriend peers similar in relational victimization instead. Relationally victimized peers may share this fear and experiences, and thus provide a safe haven for affiliation. Moreover, relational victimization is often targeted at damaging one's social relationships (Heilbron & Prinstein, 2008). If successful this can lead to more friendship de-selection over time. This de-selection effect is likely to be more visible in friendships of youth similar in relational than overt victimization due to the fear of becoming the next victim. Thus we hypothesized that similarity in friendship selection, as well as de-selection in friendships, are more pronounced in relational than overt victimization.

Overt victimization is likely to be related to stronger social influence instead. In contrast to more covert relational victimization, overt victimization is directly visible to the broader peer group and visibly damaging to the victim or his/her affiliates (Heilbron & Prinstein, 2008). Thus perceptions of overt victimization may be shared and reinforced in friendships more than those in relational victimization. Also, because bullies strive for social status (Sijtsema, Veenstra, Lindenberg, & Salmivalli, 2009), they may increasingly victimize friends of already victimized youth overtly rather than relationally because these acts are directly witnessed by other peers, thus affording admiration and social status.

THE PRESENT STUDY

Using longitudinal social network analysis (Siena; "Simulation Investigation for Empirical Network Analysis"; Steglich et al., 2010), we examined friendship selection and influence in overt and relational victimization by analyzing friendship networks in two middle schools. Recent advances in longitudinal social network analysis enable us to examine similarity in friendship selection in terms of the formation, that is, the creation as well maintenance (or termination/de-selection) of these relationships over time (Ripley, Snijders, & Preciado, 2012), while simultaneously examining social influence processes. In all analyses we adjusted for structural network parameters (the development of friendship ties) and previous friendship acquaintances (friendship length). Because friendships may already exist prior to an arbitrary first measurement, controlling for the length of friendships at T1 safeguards against inflated influence effects due to pre-existing relationships (Ojanen, Sijtsema, Hawley, & Little, 2010). Also, because friendships are largely driven by gender similarity (Hartup, 1992), we included gender in the analyses.

To summarize our hypotheses, we expected that victimization would predict selection-similarity as well as de-selection, and that friends would influence the level of victimization. However, selection-similarity was expected to be stronger in relational and social influence stronger in overt victimization. We also examined gender moderation in friendship selection and influence, which may differ for victimized boys and girls (Crick, 2010). Although findings of sex differences in relational victimization are mixed (see Heilbron & Prinstein, 2008), girls are generally more distressed by negative interpersonal events than boys (Leadbeater, Blatt, & Quinlan, 1995). Moreover, given the relative importance of social interaction in friendships for girls in particular (Hartup, 1992), especially relational victimization may evidence stronger selection and/or influence effects for girls. For boys, in turn, these processes may be more pronounced in overt victimization.

METHOD

Participants

Longitudinal survey data were collected in two middle schools in southeast Finland. At first assessment, 384 seventh and eighth grade students (12–14 years; 53% boys) consented and received parental consent to participate. Ethnic composition of the sample was 96% Finnish, 2% Russian origin, and 2% other. Participants represented various Socio-Economic Status (SES) classes with no particular emphasis on lower or higher SES. Data were collected at three occasions (T1 = March of the 7th and 8th grades, T2 = October of the 8th and 9th grades, and T3 = March of the 8th and 9th grades) at school during school hours.

Consent return rates were: T1 = 85%, T2 = 72%, and T3 = 70%. Because new participants were allowed to enter while some dropped out of the project over time, participation rates (listwise deletion for the victimization variables) varied across the measurements (T1: $N = 384$, T2: $N = 393$, and T3: $N = 310$).

Approximately 17% of the data for the original 384 participants was missing at T2, and 30% at T3. Attrition analysis indicated no mean-level differences in either form of victimization between participants who remained and those that dropped out from the study by T3. Missing data were imputed using the Expectation Maximization algorithm in SAS Proc MI (SAS Institute). Because the friendship networks included all participants who were present at one or more observations, the final sample in the longitudinal network analysis was 504. Participants could thus leave and join the networks over time, and we accounted for this by including these actors at all observations, coding them as missing when they had left or not yet joined the network. Moreover, we also included students who did not participate in any wave (6.15%) because they could also be nominated as best friends by schoolmates making them part of a friendship network. Using complete networks (i.e., full information of all network members) allowed us to examine the selection and influence processes among students more accurately (Steglich et al., 2010).

Measures

Friendship networks. At each observation participants were asked to nominate up to 18 friends from the same grade level at school. Because the data were collected at two schools and included two grade levels in each, the data included four friendship networks. Friendship networks consisting of directed friendship nominations were constructed for each school grade (1 = a given nomination, 0 = absent nomination). Values resulting from longitudinal attrition were coded as missing, which enabled us to control for actors leaving and joining the networks over time (Snijders et al., 2010).

Friendship length. Participants were asked to report the duration of each friendship at T1. Based on this information, a continuous variable was formed with values ranging from 0 (=no friendship present) to 3 (=friendship existed 6 months or longer). This variable was used in the analysis as a network covariate reflecting information about the network ties.

Overt and relational victimization. Participants rated the extent to which they felt victimized by peers. Adapted from the literature (Crick & Grotpeter, 1995), overt victimization items included: "[my peers] call me names", "[my peers] pick on me", "[my peers] hit or kick me" (T1: $\alpha = .81$; T2: $\alpha = .85$; T3: $\alpha = .80$). Relational victimization items included: "[my peers] say mean things about me", "[my peers] make fun of me" (T1: $\alpha = .81$; T2: $\alpha = .85$; T3: $\alpha = .85$). Answers were rated on a 7-point scale: 1 = (*never*)–7 = (*always*).

Confirmatory factor analysis indicated that a two-factor solution fit the data sufficiently across time: T1 = $\chi^2(384) = 1.880$, CFI = 1.00, RMSEA = .00 (.000–.050), T2 = $\chi^2(384) = 7.43$, CFI = .99, RMSEA = .05(.000–.100), T3 = $\chi^2(384) = 24.82$, CFI = .96, RMSEA = .11 (.075–.162). This solution also fit the data better than a single factor solution: T1 = $\Delta\chi^2$ (1, $N = 384$) = 21.805, $p < .001$; T2 = $\Delta\chi^2$ (1, $N = 384$) = 14.482, $p < .001$; T3 = $\Delta\chi^2$ (1, $N = 384$) = 43.380, $p < .001$. Thus overt and relational victimization represented distinct but positively correlated constructs across time (T1: $r = .83$, $p < .001$; T2: $r = .90$, $p < .001$; T3: $r = .83$, $p < .001$).

Because the EM algorithm can produce negative values (to simplify mathematical calculation; see Schafer & Graham, 2002), the original victimization scores were rounded up and added a fixed value (original score distributions retained) prior to the RSiena analyses because this software requires whole positive values as dependent variables.

Analysis strategy

Analyses were conducted using the RSiena software (Snijders et al., 2010). Before the main analyses we performed an initial test to ensure that the networks adhered to the general structure of friendship networks (e.g., positive reciprocity and transitivity; Veenstra & Steglich, 2012). In the selection analyses gender and overt and relational victimization were used as predictors and the friendship networks as dependent variables. Parameters of interest included the activity of making friendship nominations (*ego* effect), desirability as a friend (receiving nominations; *alter* effect), and similarity in friendship selection in terms of creation and endowment (maintenance) of friendship ties (Ripley et al., 2012). Accounting for ego and alter effects provides more reliable estimates of the extent to which youth formed new friendships with peers who were similar in victimization (Snijders et al., 2010). A positive creation effect implies that creation of friendships is more likely when participants are similar in victimization, whereas positive endowment reflects that friendships are likely to be maintained among youth similar in victimization. Conversely, negative endowment effects reflect de-selection or termination of friendships.

In the influence analysis friendship ties are used as predictors and victimization as the outcome. This provides information on the basic trends of change and social transmission of victimization. We considered social influence to occur when youth adjusted their own level of victimization to that of their friends, reflected by a positive parameter. For reliable estimates of social influence processes, we adjusted for the linear and quadratic shape parameter and the main effect of gender on victimization. The procedure was as follows. First, selection and influence parameters were estimated simultaneously in each network using identically specified models.

Second, these estimates were subjected to a meta-level analysis across the networks to increase the robustness of the findings (Snijders & Baerveldt, 2003). This analysis also provided information on whether parameters varied significantly across the individual networks (i.e., across school and grade level). We report meta-level estimates in this study and refer to individual networks when significant differences between grades emerged.

RESULTS

Descriptive statistics

Descriptive information on the networks and variables are presented in Table 1. On average, participants nominated five to eight friends. Friendship networks had low densities (3.7%–7.2%), or proportions of friendship nominations given, and high reciprocity and transitivity. Over 50% of the friendship nominations were reciprocated. Transitivity indexes the ratio of the number of actual and potential transitive triplets (around 40%), reflecting the tendency to nominate friends of friends also as friends. Gender similarity accounted for more than three quarters of the friendship nominations. No gender differences were observed in the level of overt or relational victimization in the networks, or across time.

To evaluate whether assessment of the co-evolution of victimization and friendship ties is feasible, Moran's *I* (network autocorrelation coefficient) was calculated to assess the degree to which friends display similarity in victimization (Veenstra & Steglich, 2012). These values were mostly positive, indicating similarity between friends; negative values or dissimilarity were observed in one network. Moreover, a sufficient fraction of stable friendship nominations (Jaccard index) is needed for longitudinal analysis (Veenstra & Steglich, 2012). This index was suitable (around 30%) in the present data.

Structural network parameters, gender, and length of friendship

Structural network parameters, reported in Table 2, indicated that friendship nominations were unlikely to occur at random (negative outdegree) and were more likely when reciprocated, or part of a transitive triplet (positive reciprocity and transitive triplets). The latter suggests that participants were likely to nominate friends of their friends also as friends. The negative three-cycles parameter indicated that friendship triplets were characterized by a hierarchical structure; that is, some participants received more friendship nominations than others within the same triplet. Moreover, youth were more likely to nominate same-sex than cross-sex peers as friends (positive same sex effect) and to nominate peers with whom they were already friends at T1 (positive friendship length effect). Taken together, the network effects

TABLE 1
Descriptive information on friendship networks, gender, and victimization variables

	School 1 Grade 7–8			*School 1 Grade 8–9*			*School 2 Grade 7–8*			*School 2 Grade 8–9*		
	T1	*T2*	*T3*	*T1*	*T2*	*T3*	*T1*	*T2*	*T3*	*T1*	*T2*	*T3*
Sample												
Cohort size	131	130	123	95	92	68	78	93	82	85	82	55
Respondents missing	15	16	23	18	21	45	41	26	37	41	44	71
fraction males	52.4%	53.1%	53.7%	48.4%	53.3%	48.5%	62.8%	55.9%	57.3%	48.2%	45.1%	36.4%
Friendship												
Average outdegree	5.33	6.22	6.65	6.21	6.09	6.93	7.41	7.45	8.44	6.92	7.57	7.04
SD outdegree	3.37	3.51	4.04	5.41	3.25	3.87	4.62	4.26	4.65	4.145	4.472	3.887
SD indegree	2.45	3.33	3.04	3.25	2.80	2.67	3.36	3.84	4.34	3.217	3.671	2.559
Density	3.7%	4.3%	4.6%	5.5%	5.4%	6.2%	6.3%	6.3%	7.2%	5.5%	6.1%	5.6%
Reciprocity	54.3%	58.2%	55.7%	51.1%	58.3%	65.8%	57.3%	60.1%	63.5%	57.5%	58.9%	54.9%
Transitivity	37.8%	42.5%	39.7%	36.9%	36.2%	43.7%	39.6%	37.8%	39.0%	32.5%	36.3%	33.8%
Same gender	89.5%	89.2%	86.6%	82.8%	82.0%	83.9%	88.0%	77.8%	77.2%	82.4%	78.3%	72.9%
Overt victimization												
Average males	4.12	4.18	3.99	4.47	4.07	4.05	4.34	4.10	4.15	4.29	4.06	4.04
Average females	4.24	4.11	3.94	3.86	3.55	3.65	3.77	3.60	3.70	4.05	3.95	4.10
SD males	1.20	1.16	0.98	1.28	0.83	1.04	1.43	1.01	1.25	1.54	1.27	1.28
SD females	1.37	1.11	1.20	1.10	0.78	0.91	1.31	0.76	1.19	1.13	0.98	1.05
Relational victimization												
Average males	4.47	4.38	4.60	4.69	4.22	4.10	4.65	4.56	4.34	4.61	4.55	3.96
Average females	4.53	4.53	4.39	4.53	4.20	4.04	4.19	3.88	3.93	4.79	4.79	4.64
SD males	1.43	1.19	1.44	1.60	0.98	1.36	1.79	1.46	1.50	1.56	1.36	1.44

(*continued*)

TABLE 1. Continued.

	School 1 Grade 7–8			*School 1 Grade 8–9*			*School 2 Grade 7–8*			*School 2 Grade 8–9*		
	T1	*T2*	*T3*	*T1*	*T2*	*T3*	*T1*	*T2*	*T3*	*T1*	*T2*	*T3*
SD females	1.53	1.46	1.45	1.38	1.44	1.36	1.42	1.01	1.35	1.62	1.42	1.14
Network autocorrelation												
Moran's *I* overt victimization	0.17	0.10	−0.06	0.08	0.06	0.08	0.04	−0.01	0.02	−0.10	−0.04	0.00
Moran's *I* relational victimization	0.06	0.10	−0.03	0.03	0.01	0.09	0.00	0.11	0.08	−0.04	−0.04	−0.04
Sample change (T)	1–2	2–3	1–3	1–2	2–3	1–3	1–2	2–3	1–3	1–2	2–3	1–3
Number leavers	0	0	0	0	0	0	0	0	0	0	0	0
Number joiners	6	0	6	5	0	5	1	2	3	1	0	1
Number stayers	140	146	140	108	113	108	116	117	116	125	126	125
Friendship change												
Distance	508	471	606	449	249	431	401	454	401	392	238	323
Jaccard index	43.3%	50.9%	38.4%	36.1%	51.9%	36.1%	43.5%	43.6%	37.3%	40.3%	47.8%	32.7%
Overt victimization change												
Distance	149	112	133	94	72	94	109	89	104	98	88	104
Fraction stable actors	35.7%	49.0%	40.6%	43.6%	47.3%	42.7%	36.0%	42.3%	40.5%	38.5%	38.5%	33.9%
Relational victimization change												
Distance	146	122	152	127	93	132	129	113	124	119	113	134
Fraction stable actors	39.9%	46.2%	39.2%	28.2%	38.2%	26.4%	31.5%	39.6%	30.6%	32.1%	31.2%	28.4%

Density was calculated as N of ties divided by the total amount of ties; Reciprocity was calculated as $2M/(2M+A)$, where M = mutual ties and A = asymmetric ties; Transitivity was calculated as N of transitive triplets divided by N of 2-paths (or 2-stars). For all network measures, structurally absent actors were excluded.

TABLE 2
Meta-level selection and influence parameters for overt and relational victimization

	Estimate	*(St. error)*	*Average SD*	χ^2
Selection Effects				
Rate of change t1–t2	11.34	(1.40)		
Rate of change t2–t3	5.74	(0.53)		
Outdegree effect on rate of change	0.01	(0.03)	0.05	1.05*
Indegree effect on rate of change	0.08	(0.03)†	0.06	6.94†
Outdegree (density)	−2.61	(0.15)***	0.31	40.25***
Reciprocity	1.70	(0.15)***	0.30	7.80*
Transitive triplets	0.39	(0.06)**	0.12	40.66***
Three-cycles	−0.37	(0.09)*	0.18	20.77***
Friendship length	0.32	(0.05)**	0.10	10.83*
Sex alter (1 = boy)	0.05	(0.03)	0.05	1.13
Sex ego	0.08	(0.08)	0.16	7.35†
Same sex	0.31	(0.08)*	0.17	14.29**
Overt victimization alter	0.07	(0.06)	0.12	5.95
Overt victimization ego	−0.08	(0.00)***	0.01	0.02
Endowment: similarity overt victimization	1.14	(1.72)	3.45	8.47*
Creation: similarity overt victimization	−1.10	(1.12)	2.25	4.33
Similarity × sex ego	0.51	(0.27)	0.54	0.44
Relational victimization alter	−0.08	(0.02)*	0.04	1.67
Relational victimization ego	0.05	(0.00)***	0.00	0.02
Endowment: similarity relational victimization	0.10	(0.22)	0.44	0.30
Creation: similarity relational victimization	1.46	(0.43)*	0.85	0.84
Similarity × sex ego	−0.49	(0.76)	1.52	4.24
Influence: Overt victimization				
Rate of change t1–t2	3.78	(0.39)		
Rate of change t2–t3	2.72	(0.17)		
Linear shape	−0.08	(0.04)	0.07	2.71
Quadratic shape	−0.08	(0.02)*	0.04	0.46
Similarity in overt victimization	6.32	(0.89)**	1.79	0.91
Effect from sex	0.09	(0.07)	0.14	2.25
Similarity × sex	−2.27	(2.38)	4.75	5.29
Influence: Relational victimization				
Rate of change t1–t2	4.21	(0.29)		
Rate of change t2–t3	3.24	(0.40)		
Linear shape	−0.05	(0.02)	0.04	1.86
Quadratic shape	−0.04	(0.02)	0.04	1.09
Similarity in relational victimization	4.69	(0.74)**	1.47	0.92
Effect from sex	0.02	(0.07)	0.14	4.50
Similarity × sex	−1.68	(1.01)	2.02	2.06

†$p \leq .10$, *$p \leq .05$, **$p \leq .01$, ***$p \leq .001$; two-tailed tests.
Significance testing was not performed for the Rate of change effects because the null-hypothesis would imply no changes (which was not the case). X^2 test of variance according to Snijders and Baerveldt (2003) method.

imply that participants had a tendency to keep the friendship networks closed.

Overt and relational victimization: Friendship selection and influence

Meta-level selection and influence parameters for overt and relational victimization are reported in Table 2. Chi-square tests indicate whether effects differed per school grade. Higher chi-square values indicate more pronounced differences between school grades. When there were significant differences we discuss these in the text. Effects were estimated for overt and relational victimization separately and simultaneously. However, because the results did not differ substantially, we only present the models where we analyzed both types of victimization simultaneously.

Ego effects of overt victimization indicated that participants who were higher on overt victimization were less likely to nominate friends ("lower" activity in the networks; negative ego effect). In contrast to our hypothesis we found no support for friendship selection on the basis of overt victimization. However, there were significant differences between grade networks with regard to the maintenance of friendship ties (endowment similarity effect; $X^2 = 8.47$, $df = 3$, $p < .05$). Closer inspection of these networks (tables not reported here) indicated that in the older cohort at school 1 (in grade 8 at T1), youth were more likely to maintain friendship ties with those similar in overt victimization (endowment similarity effect; Est. = 4.39, $SE = 1.86$, $p < .05$). However, in the younger cohort in school 1, youth were more likely to terminate friendships when they were similar in overt victimization (Est. = −3.30, $SE = 1.97$, $p < .10$).

Also reported in Table 2, adolescents high on relational victimization were less likely to be nominated as friends (lower "undesirability" as a friend; negative alter effect) and more likely to extend friendship nominations to others (higher "activity" in the networks; positive ego effect) than those low on relational victimization. Moreover, a positive similarity creation effect indicated that youth high on relational victimization were likely to extend friendship nominations to peers who experienced similar levels of relational victimization. Given the non-significant endowment effect, the findings indicate that similarity in relational victimization between friends was driven by establishment rather than maintenance of these relationships. No gender differences were observed for either form of victimization.

Social influence effects are also reported in Table 2. As indicated by the negative quadratic shape, the development of overt victimization followed a curvilinear trend: youth with higher initial overt victimization scores decreased and those with lower initial scores increased in overt victimization over time (a self-correcting effect, or regression to the mean).

Moreover, a positive similarity effect provided evidence for social influence: adolescents grew increasingly similar to their friends in overt victimization over time. Development of relational victimization could not be modeled by a linear or quadratic shape. However, the positive similarity effect provided support for social influence in relational victimization.

DISCUSSION

In this study we examined friendship selection, de-selection, and social influence in the development of overt and relational victimization during middle school. In line with our *selection hypothesis*, we found that friendship formation was driven by similarity in relational victimization. However, mixed support was found with regard to overt victimization in this respect. In one friendship network in one grade friendship formation was driven by similarity in overt victimization, but in another network in another grade friendships between overtly victimized adolescents were dissolved over time (*de-selection* of similar friends). Moreover, in line with the *social influence hypothesis*, friends grew similar to each other in both relational and overt victimization. These selection, de-selection, and influence processes were similar for boys and girls. To the best of our knowledge, the findings provide the first evidence for friendship selection and influence in adolescent victimization and are discussed in light of implications that for research on bullying and victimization in middle school.

Overt and relational victimization: Friendship selection, de-selection, and influence

Overt victimization was negatively and relational victimization positively related to extending friendship nominations to others. Although we did not expect overt and relational victimization to differ in the direction of effects, these findings suggest that overtly victimized adolescents are passive in making new friends while relationally victimized youth actively seek new friends. This implies that overtly victimized youth keep their situation unchanged (even when suffering from the lack or stability of friendships), whereas relationally victimized youth try to overcome their negative experiences by making friends. The latter is consistent with the observed negative effect of receiving friendship nominations from others in relational victimization: because relationally victimized youth are unattractive as friends, they may also need to be more active in establishing these relationships themselves. Collectively these findings suggest that relational more than overt victimization is related to difficulties in establishing friendships and align with the idea relational victimization is a risk factor for the establishment of these important relationships (see also Eslea et al., 2004).

Relational victimization also evidenced selection-similarity in friendships. That is, adolescents selected friends who were similar in relational victimization across all individual networks in this study. This supports the default-selection hypothesis proposing that victimized adolescents befriend each other for lacking alternative friendship options (Deptula & Cohen, 2004; Sijtsema et al., 2010) as well as our hypothesis concerning stronger selection-similarity in friendships for relationally than overtly victimized youth. Specifically, it may be that relationally victimized youth resort to befriending similarly victimized peers more than those dissimilar in this respect because they fear the consequences of potential relational victimization in relationships with peers who may not be victimized themselves.

Overt victimization was unrelated to selection-similarity in friendships. Findings for friendship maintenance and termination (de-selection) were mixed and should be interpreted with caution. In one friendship network overt victimization was related to maintenance of friendships, whereas in another friendship network it was related to de-selection or terminating friendships. Maintenance processes are positive indicators of stability in friendships for overtly victimized youth, assuming that these relationships provide emotional benefits rather than adjustment difficulties. De-selection processes, in turn, may reflect poor social skills (Fox & Boulton, 2006), rejection (Hodges et al., 1997), and friendship conflicts (Bagwell & Schmidt, 2011) among victimized youth, or may reflect fear of further victimization in relationships with similarly overtly victimized youth. While discrepant findings across individual friendship networks seem confusing, these may reflect social-contextual processes within peer groups. Specifically, previous studies have shown that specific contexts and group norms can have a crucial impact on the relationship between victimization and social adjustment (Huitsing, Veenstra, Sainio, & Salmivalli, in press; Sentse Scholte, Salmivalli, & Voeten, 2007). However, more conclusive evidence is needed to support the idea of maintenance and de-selection of friendships with regard to overt victimization.

Although we expected to observe friendship de-selection for both forms of victimization, this process was only observed for overt victimization, in one friendship network. Given that relational victimization was neither related to maintaining nor dissolving friendships, it is unclear whether friendships of relationally victimized youth are stable or frequently dissolved. Psychological or contextual variables may show opposite effects in this respect depending on, for instance, whether relational victimization is related to friendship quality (e.g., differences in friendship conflicts may produce differences in friendship stability; Bagwell & Schmidt, 2011).

As expected, the development of overt and relational victimization both depended on social influence. That is, adolescent friends grew increasingly similar in their experiences of overt as well as relational victimization during middle school. Friends of victimized youth who were originally below the mean on either form of victimization reported increasing victimization over time, but those who were above the mean on victimization reported decreasing levels of victimization over time in correspondence to their friends' level of victimization. To the best of our knowledge this provides the first developmental evidence indicating that having victimized friends may increase the risk of future victimization and augments cross-sectional findings on matching levels of friends' victimization and one's own rejection by peers (Ray et al., 1997). On the up side, friendships among victimized youth also involved social influence in the positive direction (i.e., decreasing levels of victimization over time). Thus, our findings align with existing findings on both positive (Adams et al., 2011; Wang et al., 2009) and negative (Fox & Boulton, 2006; Hodges et al., 1999) effects of friendships for victimized youth. Previous studies suggest that these protective effects of friendships depend to a large extent on whether friendships are of high quality; that is, involve intimacy, trust, fun, and low levels of conflict (Hartup, 1992; Hodges et al., 1999).

In a previous study we focused on the extent to which adolescents were (relationally or overtly) aggressive themselves (Sijtsema, Ojanen, et al., 2010). Interestingly, there is an important difference between the perpetrators and the victims of aggression (although for some, these roles may co-occur). That is, with regard to the perpetrators of aggression the prior study found support for social influence with regard to relational, but not overt aggression. Together with the current finding that friends influence overt victimization, it is tempting to speculate that overt aggression is socially negatively perceived. On the one hand, the benefits of becoming more similar to overtly aggressive friends are low. On the other hand, youth who affiliate with overtly victimized peers may become more overtly victimized themselves. At this time, little is known about the processes that may account for social influence in victimization. The direction of influence may depend on whether friendships are of high quality, or are in support of co-rumination and thus have aversive effects on well-being (Hartup, 1992; Rose et al., 2007). Moreover, the marginal status of victimized youth can spread over to friends who may be at higher risk for victimization for affiliating with other victimized youth.

Implications, limitations, and directions for future research

Conceptually, the present findings indicate that victimized youth have challenges in friendships and suggest that it is fruitful to examine overt and relational forms of victimization separately to understand friendships of victimized youth in more depth. The findings support tailored bullying interventions separated by the behavioral form of these behaviors (Leff, Waasdorp, & Crick, 2010), given that the adjustment difficulties victimized youth experience may depend on the way bullying occurs. The present findings indicate that especially relationally victimized youth experience difficulties in establishing friendships. Methodologically, the strengths of this study include the assessment of friendship networks based on school grades rather than a more limited class context, as well as assessment of similarity in friendship selection in terms of creation and maintenance (endowment) of friendships over time (Veenstra & Dijkstra, 2011). Our findings advance research utilizing this novel approach to social network analysis, suggesting that it is worthwhile to assess these processes separately.

This study had some limitations. First, the present data did not include information on friendship quality, which can affect adjustment beyond the number of friends (Hartup, 1992). Assessment of friendship quality would be worthwhile as it could explain why adolescents maintain or terminate friendships with equally victimized peers. Second, our data was limited to self-reported victimization. Although self-reports are meaningful, particularly in the study of relational victimization that may be less visible to the broader peer group or teachers, views on the best assessment of victimization vary (see Sainio et al., 2011). For a more comprehensive view on social influence in victimization, the present analyses should be replicated using peer-reported overt and relational victimization. Third, it would be meaningful to examine friendships that victimized youth may have outside of the school context. While most friendships are sought at school, youth usually have friends elsewhere as well (Kiesner, Poulin, & Nicotra, 2003). These relationships may provide support and have differential implications for adjustment especially for youth who are victimized in school.

Despite the limitations, this study is the first to examine friendship selection and social influence in victimization. The findings suggest that victimized youth may have difficulties in friendships, victimization largely depends on social influence among adolescent friends, and that it is worthwhile to consider overt and relational victimization separately to understand the development of victimization in more depth. Future research would benefit from assessing social influence concurrently with friendship quality and social contextual factors that may help us to understand social influence in victimization in more detail.

REFERENCES

Adams, R. E., Santo, J. B., & Bukowski, W. M. (2011). The presence of a best friend buffers the effects of negative experiences. *Developmental Psychology*, *47*(6), 1786–1791, doi:10.1037/a0025401.

Bagwell, C. L., & Schmidt, M. E. (2011). The friendship quality of overtly and relationally victimized children. *Merrill-Palmer Quarterly-Journal of Developmental Psychology*, *57*(2), 158–185.

Crick, N. R. (2010). The role of overt aggression, relational aggression, and prosocial behavior in the prediction of children's future social adjustment. *Child Development*, *67*(5), 2317–2327.

Crick, N., Casas, J., & Nelson, D. (2002). Toward a more comprehensive understanding of peer maltreatment: Studies of relational victimization. *Current Directions in Psychological Science*, *11*(3), 98–101, doi:10.1111/1467-8721.00177.

Crick, N. R., & Grotpeter, J. K. (1995). Relational aggression, gender, and social-psychological adjustment. *Child Development*, *66*(3), 710–722.

Crick, N., & Nelson, D. (2002). Relational and physical victimization within friendships: Nobody told me there'd be friends like these. *Journal of Abnormal Child Psychology*, *30*(6), 599–607, doi:10.1023/A:1020811714064.

Crick, N. R., Nelson, D. A., Morales, J. R., Cullerton-Sen, C., Casas, J. F., & Hickman, S. (2001). Relational victimization in childhood and adolescence: I hurt you through the grapevine. In J. Juvonen & S. Graham (Eds.), *School-based peer harassment: The plight of the vulnerable and victimized* (pp. 196–214). New York: Guilford Press.

Deptula, D. P., & Cohen, R. (2004). Aggressive, rejected, and delinquent children and adolescents: A comparison of their friendships. *Aggression and Violent Behavior*, *9*(1), 75–104.

Dishion, T. J., Piehler, T. F., & Myers, M. W. (2008). Dynamics and ecology of adolescent peer influences. In M. J. Prinstein & K. A. Dodge (Eds.), *Understanding peer influence in children and adolescents* (pp. 72–93). New York: Guilford Press.

Eslea, M., Menesini, E., Morita, Y., O'Moore, M., Mora-Merchan, J., Pereira, B., et al. (2004). Friendship and loneliness among bullies and victims: Data from seven countries. *Aggressive Behavior*, *30*(1), 71–83, doi:10.1002/ab.20006.

Fox, C., & Boulton, M. (2006). Friendship as a moderator of the relationship between social skills problems and peer victimization. *Aggressive Behavior*, *32*(2), 110–121, doi:10.1002/ab.20114.

Hartup, W. W. (1992). Friendships and their developmental significance. In H. McGurk (Ed.), *Childhood social development: Contemporary perspectives* (pp. 175–205). Hillsdale, NJ: Lawrence Erlbaum Associates Inc.

Heilbron, N., & Prinstein, M. (2008). A review and reconceptualization of social aggression: Adaptive and maladaptive correlates. *Clinical Child and Family Psychology Review*, *11*(4), 176–217.

Hodges, E. V. E., Boivin, M., Vitaro, F., & Bukowski, W. M. (1999). The power of friendship: Protection against an escalating cycle of peer victimization. *Developmental Psychology*, *35*(1), 94–101.

Hodges, E. V. E., Malone, M., & Perry, D. (1997). Individual risk and social risk as interacting determinants of victimization in the peer group. *Developmental Psychology*, *33*(6), 1032–1039, doi:10.1037/0012-1649.33.6.1032.

Huitsing, G., Veenstra, R., Sainio, M., & Salmivalli, C. (in press). "It must be me" or "It could be them?" The impact of the social network position of bullies and victims on victims' adjustment. *Social Networks,* doi:10.1016/j.socnet.2010.07.002.

Kandel, D. B. (1978). Homophily, selection, and socialization in adolescent friendships. *American Journal of Sociology*, *84*(2), 427–436.

Kiesner, J., Poulin, F., & Nicotra, E. (2003). Peer relations across contexts: Individual-network homophily and network inclusion in and after school. *Child Development*, *74*(5), 1328–1343.

Leadbeater, B., Blatt, S., & Quinlan, D. (1995). Gender-linked vulnerabilities to depressive symptoms, stress, and problem behaviors in adolescents. *Journal of Research on Adolescence*, *5*(1), 1–29, doi:10.1207/s15327795jra0501_1.

Leff, S. S., Waasdorp, T. E., & Crick, N. R. (2010). A review of existing relational aggression programs: Strengths, limitations, and future directions. *School Psychological Review*, *39*(4), 508–535.

Lindenberg, S. (1996). Continuities in the theory of social production functions. In H. Ganzeboom & S. Lindenberg (Eds.), *Verklarende sociologie. Opstellen voor Reinhard Wippler* (pp. 169–184). Amsterdam: Thesis Publishers.

Marsh, P., Allen, J. P., Ho, M., Porter, M., & McFarland, F. C. (2006). The changing nature of adolescent friendships – longitudinal links with early adolescent ego development. *Journal of Early Adolescence*, *26*(4), 414–431.

McPherson, M., Smith-Lovin, L., & Cook, J. M. (2001). Birds of a feather: Homophily and social networks. *Annual Review of Sociology*, *27*, 415–444.

Mouttapa, M., Valente, T., Gallaher, P., Rohrbach, L., & Unger, J. (2004). Social network predictors of bullying and victimization. *Adolescence*, *39*(154), 315–335.

Newcomb, A. F., & Bagwell, C. L. (1995). Children's friendship relations: A meta-analytic review. *Psychological Bulletin*, *117*, 306–347.

Ojanen, T., Sijtsema, J. J., Hawley, P. H., & Little, T. D. (2010). Intrinsic and extrinsic motivation in early adolescents' friendship development: Friendship selection, influence, and prospective friendship quality. *Journal of Adolescence*, *33*(6), 837–851, doi:10.1016/j.adolescence.2010.08.004.

Pendell, S. D. (2002). Affection in interpersonal relationships: Not just "a fond or tender feeling". *Communication Yearbook*, *26*, 70–115.

Ray, G., Cohen, R., Secrist, M., & Duncan, M. (1997). Relating aggressive and victimization behaviors to children's sociometric status and friendships. *Journal of Social and Personal Relationships*, *14*(1), 95–108, doi:10.1177/0265407597141005.

Reijntjes, A., Kamphuis, J. H., Prinzie, P., & Telch, M. J. (2010). Peer victimization and internalizing problems in children: A meta-analysis of longitudinal studies. *Child Abuse & Neglect*, *34*(4), 244–252, doi:10.1016/j.chiabu.2009.07.009.

Ripley, R. M., Snijders, T. A. B., & Preciado, P. (2012). *Manual for RSiena.* Oxford, UK: Department of Statistics, Nuffield College.

Rose, A. J., Carlson, W., & Waller, E. M. (2007). Prospective associations of co-rumination with friendship and emotional adjustment: Considering the socioemotional trade-offs of co-rumination. *Developmental Psychology*, *43*(4), 1019–1031.

Sainio, M., Veenstra, R., Huitsing, G., & Salmivalli, C. (2011). Victims and their defenders: A dyadic approach. *International Journal of Behavioral Development*, *35*(2), 144–151, doi:10.1177/0165025410378068.

Salmivalli, C., & Peets, K. (2009). Pre-adolescents' peer-relational schemas and social goals across relational contexts. *Social Development*, *18*(4), 817–832, doi:10.1111/j.1467-9507.2008.00515.x.

Schafer, J., & Graham, J. (2002). Missing data: Our view of the state of the art. *Psychological Methods*, *7*(2), 147–177, doi:10.1037//1082-989X.7.2.147.

Sentse, M., Scholte, R., Salmivalli, C., & Voeten, M. (2007). Person-group dissimilarity in involvement in bullying and its relation with social status. *Journal of Abnormal Child Psychology*, *35*(6), 1009–1019.

Sijtsema, J. J., Lindenberg, S., & Veenstra, R. (2010). Testing homophily against default selection in friendships of overtly aggressive early adolescents: Do they get what they want or are they stuck with what they can get? *Journal of Abnormal Child Psychology*, *38*(6), 803–817.

Sijtsema, J. J., Ojanen, T., Veenstra, R., Lindenberg, S. M., Hawley, P. H., & Little, T. D. (2010). Functions and forms of aggression in adolescent friendship selection and influence: A longitudinal social network analysis. *Social Development*, *19*, 515–534.

Sijtsema, J. J., Veenstra, R., Lindenberg, S., & Salmivalli, C. (2009). Empirical test of bullies' status goals: Assessing direct goals, aggression, and prestige. *Aggressive Behavior*, *35*, 57–67.

Snijders, T. A. B., & Baerveldt, C. (2003). A multilevel network study of the effects of delinquent behavior on friendship evolution. *Journal of Mathematical Sociology*, *27*(2–3), 123–151.

Snijders, T. A. B., van de Bunt, G. G., & Steglich, C. E. G. (2010). Introduction to stochastic actor-based models for network dynamics. *Social Networks*, *32*(1), 44–60, doi:10.1016/j.socnet.2009.02.004.

Steglich, C., Snijders, T. A. B., & Pearson, M. (2010). Dynamic networks and behavior: Separating selection from influence. *Sociological Methodology*, *40*, 329–393, doi:10.1111/j.1467-9531.2010.01225.x.

Veenstra, R., & Dijkstra, J. K. (2011). Transformations in adolescent peer networks. In B. Laursen & W. A. Collins (Eds.), *Relationship pathways: From adolescence to young adulthood* (pp. 135–154). Los Angeles: Sage.

Veenstra, R., & Steglich, C. E. G. (2012). Actor-based model for network and behavior dynamics. In B. Laursen, T. D. Little, & N. A. Card (Eds.), *Handbook of developmental research methods* (pp. 598–618). New York: Guilford Press.

Wang, J., Iannotti, R. J., & Nansel, T. R. (2009). School bullying among adolescents in the United States: Physical, verbal, relational, and cyber. *Journal of Adolescent Health*, *45*(4), 368–375, doi:10.1016/j.jadohealth.2009.03.021.

Social context of bullying: Do misperceptions of group norms influence children's responses to witnessed episodes?

Marlene Sandstrom[1], Heather Makover[1], and Maria Bartini[2]
[1]Department of Psychology, Williams College, Williamstown, MA, USA
[2]Department of Psychology, Massachusetts College of Liberal Arts, North Adams, MA, USA

This study explores the association between norm misperception and behavioral responses to witnessed bullying episodes. We hypothesized that pluralistic ignorance (PI) could explain individual differences in behavioral responses. According to PI theory, children who believe that victims deserve protection may inhibit defending behavior if they assume their attitudes are out of step with their peers. A total of 446 fourth and eighth graders described their personal attitudes and perceptions of peers' attitudes about bullying, as well as their behavioral responses when they witnessed a bullying episode. Consistent with PI theory, children perceived their personal attitudes as more prosocial than those of their classmates. Further, misperception of group norms was associated with children's reports of behavioral responses to bullying; children who overestimated peers' approval of bullying reported lower levels of defending the victim and higher levels of joining in.

A large percentage of children serve as witnesses to bullying episodes, without getting involved to defend the victim or stop the bully (Salmivalli, Lagerspetz, Björkqvist, Osterman, & Kaukiainen 1996). One explanation

This material is based on work supported by the National Science Foundation under Grant No. 0841897. The authors are grateful to the students, teachers, and school administrators who participated in this study. We extend special thanks to Meredith Craven, Meg Macdonald, and Colleen Fitzpatrick, who helped to orchestrate the data collection process.

for inaction may be that latent inclinations to defend victims are inhibited by perceptions that there is group support for bullies (e.g., Pozzoli & Gini, 2010; Swearer, Espelage, Vaillancourt, & Hymel, 2010). In the current study we examine the association between children's perceptions of group norms about bullying and their typical responses when they witness bullying at school.

BEYOND BULLIES AND VICTIMS

Bullying is generally defined as aggression by a person of greater power towards a person with less power, and can take the form of verbal, physical, relational, or cyber attacks (Olweus & Limber, 2007). It is important to recognize, however, that bullying involves many more people than just the bully and victim. Often bullying occurs in front of a group of peers. Salmivalli and colleagues (1996) studied the behavioral responses children enact in bullying situations, and found that 87% of students could be labeled as taking part in the process in some fashion, either as *Bully*, *Assistant*, *Reinforcer*, *Defender*, or *Bystander*. In a naturalistic study O'Connell, Pepler, and Craig (1999) examined peers' behavioral reactions to live bullying episodes. Close analysis of 53 videotaped episodes from the playground revealed that onlookers actively reinforced bullies 21% of the time, passively reinforced bullies by standing and watching 54% of the time, and intervened to support victims only 25% of the time. These results demonstrate that peers play a central role in bullying, and are most likely to behave in ways that overtly or tacitly support the bully.

In another naturalistic study, Hawkins, Pepler, and Craig (2001) examined the frequency, nature, and effectiveness of peer intervention strategies in bullying situations. A focal sample of children identified by peers as bullies and victims were videotaped during recess over the course of 3 years. Footage revealed that while peers were present for 88% of bullying episodes, they chose to intervene only 19% of the time. Interestingly these interventions (though low-frequency occurrences) were successful in stopping ongoing acts of bullying over two-thirds of the time (Hawkins et al., 2001). This finding underscores the efficacy of peer intervention, and leads to the question: If peer intervention works so well, why do children who witness bullying typically choose to remain passive?

ATTITUDES ABOUT BULLIES AND VICTIMS

A parsimonious explanation for peer passivity in the face of bullying is that children condone (or at least do not actively disapprove of) bullying. Indeed, there is research to suggest that some children who witness peers being bullied report high levels of moral disengagement and indicate that they do not feel any responsibility to help (e.g., Obermann, 2011). A consistent body of research, however, documents that many students do not hold such views. In contrast, many children indicate that they are opposed to bullies, support victims, and feel that intervening to stop bullying is the right thing to do (e.g., Boulton, Bucci, & Hawker, 1999; Charach, Pepler, & Ziegler, 1995; Eslea & Smith, 2000; Hymel, Schonert-Reichl, Bonanno, Vaillancourt, & Henderson, 2010; Menesini et al., 1997; Rigby & Slee, 1993).

PERCEPTION OF GROUP NORMS

If children are personally neither apathetic nor approving of bullying, other processes must be at play to maintain their passivity. Indeed, there are many additional contributors to passivity, including fear of retaliation, self-efficacy, self-esteem, empathy, disengagement, behavioral skill at defending, and level of status within the peer group (e.g., Gini, Albiero, Benelli, & Altoe, 2008; Gini, Pozzoli, Borghi, & Franzoni, 2008; Mishna & Alaggia, 2005; Poyhonen, Juvonen, & Salmivalli, 2010; Salmivalli, Kaukiainen, Kaistaniemi, & Lagerspetz, 1999; Sentse, Scholte, Salmivalli, & Voeten, 2007; Twemlow, Fonagy, & Sacco, 2010). An additional factor that is known to have enormous influence on social behavior is group norms. Research has shown that social context plays an important role in determining children's responses to observed bullying at school.

For example, Pozzoli and Gini (2010) found that children's perceptions of normative pressure from the peer group to intervene on behalf of victims were positively associated with defending behavior, and negatively associated with passive behavior. Notably, perceived peer normative pressure also moderated the association between personal responsibility and behavior. Children who perceived a high level of peer pressure to intervene reported higher levels of defending behavior regardless of their personal attitudes about intervention; even students' with low personal responsibility toward victims reported higher levels of defending behavior when they believed that other classmates expected it. When perceived pressure for intervention was low, however, the expected association between personal responsibility toward victims and self-reported defending behavior emerged.

In a related study, Salmivalli and Voeten (2004) examined the association between perceived group norms and children's behavioral responses when they witnessed bullying. Participants' perceptions of how the group would respond to bullying episodes explained a significant amount of variance in how they responded to peer harassment, even after controlling for personal attitudes.

BYSTANDER BEHAVIOR MAY SHAPE PERCEPTIONS OF GROUP NORMS

Little is known about how children determine the relevant norms about bullying in their respective groups. In one attempt to explore how children interpret the bullying episodes they observe, Gini and colleagues (2008) asked children what they inferred from classmates' reactions to observed bullying, and then examined what influence these inferences had on participants' own perceptions and behaviors. Participants were asked to read about a bullying episode involving a group of onlookers who responded in one of three ways: watching passively, joining the bully, or defending the victim. Participants then rated how much they supported the bystanders' behavior and how much they liked or blamed the victim.

Overall, participants expressed support for the prosocial behavior of defenders, and disapproved of those who joined the bully or passively watched the situation. However, children reported more blame and less liking of victims when bullying occurred in the context of bystander passivity. This finding suggests that contextual cues may play a key role in shaping perceived norms. Children may notice classmates' passivity, and then draw an erroneous inference about their attitudes (e.g., *My classmates are passive because they believe that bullying is acceptable, or that this victim deserves poor treatment*).

THE CONCEPT OF PLURALISTIC IGNORANCE

The notion that children may misperceive group *attitudes* toward bullies and victims by making erroneous inferences on the basis of group *behavior* resonates with a large social psychological literature on *pluralistic ignorance*. Pluralistic ignorance (PI) is the process by which people act in opposition to their privately held beliefs in order to avoid social discomfort, while simultaneously assuming that the behavior of everyone else is a direct reflection of their privately held beliefs (Miller & McFarland, 1991).

PI might apply to children's perceptions of how their classmates feel about bullies and victims. When children witness a bullying incident they typically see additional observers passively standing by. Although bystanders may be aware that their own private beliefs (e.g., empathy for the victim; disapproval toward the bully) are at odds with passive, unhelpful behavior, the theory of PI would suggest that they do not grant others this same possibility. Instead they erroneously conclude that the other bystanders are passive because they hold less-prosocial attitudes (i.e., believe that some kids deserve to bullied, or that defending a victim is a bad idea). As a result children perceive their own private (prosocial) beliefs to be markedly out of step with those of their peers. This miscalculation about group consensus may lead children to restrain their own helping behavior.

In contrast, children who believe their classmates share their "pro" defending views might expect peers to come to their aid when they stand up to a bully, leading to heightened efficacy, less fear of rejection, and more helping behavior.

PI AND BEHAVIORAL RESPONSES TO WITNESSED BULLYING

To date, only one study has examined the association between PI and behavioral responses to witnessed bullying (Sandstrom & Bartini, 2010). In this study a sample of eighth graders described their personal attitudes, as well as their perceptions of group attitudes about bullies and victims. In addition teachers rated the frequency with which participants joined in the bullying, stood by passively, or defended victims when they witnessed acts of bullying. Results indicated that children *did* perceive themselves as holding *more* prosocial attitudes about bullying than their peers, confirming the premise that PI emerges in the context of attitudes toward bullying. In order to determine whether norm misperception was associated with children's behavioral responses to witnessed bulling, we computed misperception as a "discrepancy" or "bias" score (i.e., the *difference* between the level of prosocial attitude reflected in children's personal rating versus their perception of their classmates' ratings). Results provided partial support for the theoretical model described here. There was a positive association between norm misperception and passively standing by when bullying occurred. Specifically, eighth graders who perceived themselves as holding more prosocial attitudes than their peers were described by their teachers as engaging in higher levels of passivity when they witnessed bullying. Contrary to predictions, however, the negative association between misperception and defending behavior failed to emerge.

One limitation of this study was the operational definition of misperception. The use of a difference score (level of one's own prosocial attitude versus perception of classmates' prosocial attitude) has been used elsewhere in the PI literature (e.g., Shelton & Richeson, 2005), and reflects the extent to which individuals view their own attitudes as more prosocial than those of their classmates. What PI does *not* reflect, however, is the extent to which individuals are actually *misperceiving* the group norm. An individual discrepancy between one's personal attitude and one's perception of classmates' attitudes need not imply a misperception of the group norm (i.e., an individual could hold an accurate perception of the group attitude, while simultaneously believing that his personal attitude is significantly more prosocial than that norm). An alternative method for calculating misperception of norms involves computing the discrepancy between the *actual* classroom norm (i.e., the mean personal attitude score of all members of the group) and the individual's *perception* of that group norm.

This operational definition, adopted in the current study, has been used extensively in the PI literature (e.g., LaBrie, Hummer, Grant, & Lac, 2010; LaBrie, Hummer, Neighbors, & Pedersen, 2008).

A second explanation for the lack of association between PI and behavioral responses to witnessed bullying in the previous study may hinge on its reliance on teachers as primary informants on participants' responses to bullying events. Prior research has demonstrated that much of the aggressive behavior that occurs at school unfolds in contexts where teachers and other adult observers are not present (Pellegrini & Bartini, 2000). Therefore the current study uses self-report measures of participant role in order to capture children's behavioral responses to *all* instances in which children witness peer mistreatment, rather than only the subset of such episodes that are observed by the classroom teacher.

THE CURRENT STUDY

The purpose of the current study is (1) to replicate preliminary findings documenting the applicability of pluralistic ignorance (PI) to the context of bullying, (2) to explore potential age and gender differences in the expression of PI by including both primary and middle school populations, and (3) to examine the association between actual *misperception* of norms and children's behavioral responses to witnessed bullying.

Based on prior literature and theoretical considerations, we made three preliminary predictions. First, we expected PI to emerge in the context of witnessing bullying. We predicted that, overall, participants would view their own attitudes about bullies, victims, and defending attempts as systematically more prosocial than those of their classmates.

Second, we expected individual differences PI to vary as a function of gender and age. Sandstrom and Bartini (2010) found that eighth-grade girls exhibited higher levels of PI than boys in the context of bullying. A similar gender difference in PI has been found in the domain of alcohol consumption; females perceive a greater discrepancy between private and group attitudes about drinking than males do (e.g., Hines, Saris, & Throckmorton-Belzer, 2002; Prentice & Miller, 1993). We expected to replicate this gender difference in the current study. In addition, we speculated that the manifestation of PI might differ as a function of age. To date there have been no cross-sectional studies of PI. However, developmental increases in the ability to mask private attitudes and emotions (e.g., Saarni, 1988), as well as in the tendency to use social comparisons when evaluating the self (e.g., Ruble, Boggiano, Feldman, & Loebl, 1980), led us to expect higher levels of PI among eighth graders than fourth graders.

Third, we expected misperception of group norms to be associated with participants' behaviorial responses to witnessed bullying episodes.

The theory of PI suggests that, when children misperceive group attitudes, they will constrain their own behavior to fit their mistaken perceptions of the larger group. Therefore we expected children who underestimated the extent to which their classmates held prosocial values (i.e., disapproval for bullying, admiration for defenders) to report engaging in fewer active helping behaviors, and more passive watching behaviors when they witnessed peer mistreatment at school. Although we had no a priori assumptions about the role of age and gender in the association between children's misperceptions of their classmates' attitudes and their own behavioral responses, we included both variables as potential moderators.

METHOD

Participants

The sample included a total of 446 participants, including 90 female and 89 male fourth graders, and 134 female and 133 male eighth graders from three public school districts in rural New England. All participating schools were similar in socioeconomic status and ethnic demographics. The percentage of students who qualified for free or reduced-price lunches in these districts ranged from 12% to 22%; the percentage of non-white students ranged from 9% to 11%. Parental informed consent forms were sent to the parents of all fourth and eighth graders in participating schools (200 fourth graders and 292 eighth graders); only those students who provided signed parental consent and personal assent participated in the study. Final participation rate was 90% for fourth graders and 91% for eighth graders.

Procedure

Participants completed a survey that asked about their personal attitudes about bullies and victims, as well as their perceptions of their *peers'* attitudes about bullies and victims. Participants also rated their behavioral response style (e.g., bully, defender, bystander) when they witnessed bullying episodes. No standard definition of bullying was provided to participants; they answered all questions based on their personal understanding of the construct.

Measures

Attitudes. Personal attitudes were measured through an adapted version of Hymel, Rocke-Henderson, and Bonanno's (2005) scale, by asking participants to evaluate the extent to which they agreed with 10 statements about bullies, victims, and attempts to intervene when bullying occurs. Some items reflected an antisocial attitude (e.g., "*Kids who get bullied usually deserve it*"; "*When a bully is picking on somebody, it is OK to stand there and watch*"), while others reflected a prosocial attitude (e.g., "*I respect kids who try to stop bullying*"; "*Bullying any kid is wrong, even kids I don't like*"). Higher scores on all items indicated greater agreement with the statement. We reverse scored items that were phrased as antisocial attitudes. Therefore higher scores on all items indicated more agreement with prosocial attitudes and/or more disagreement with antisocial attitudes. Similarly, lower scores indicated more agreement with antisocial items and/or disagreement with prosocial items.

In keeping with prior research on social norms estimation (e.g., Prentice & Miller, 1993; Shelton & Richeson, 2005), participants were asked to rate the extent to which they *personally* agreed with each statement (i.e., "*me* statements"), and then rate the extent to which they thought most *other kids in their grade* would agree with each statement (i.e., "*them* statements") on a 4-point Likert scale ranging from 1 (strongly agree) to 4 (strongly disagree). Items measuring personal attitudes ("*me*" statements) resulted in an α of .83; items measuring the perceptions of others' beliefs ("*them*" statements) also resulted in an α of .83. We computed the average across all "me" statements to create a composite "me" attitude score, and an average across all "them" statements to create a composite "them" attitude score. In both cases higher scores indicated more prosocial attitudes (e.g., greater disapproval of bulling, empathy for the victim, and respect for defending behaviors), while lower scores indicated more antisocial attitudes on these dimensions.

Behavioral response to witnessed bullying. The second part of the questionnaire included a self-report adaptation of the Participant Role Questionnaire (Salmivalli et al., 1996) designed to assess how often children enacted particular behavioral responses when exposed to bullying incidents at school. Previous research comparing children's self-reported roles in bullying episodes with peer nominations indicates adequate overlap between peer- and self-reports (Belacchi, 2008; Salmivalli et al., 1996).

The original questionnaire consisted of five subscales: Bully (e.g., *How often have you started the bullying?*), Assistant (e.g., *How often have you helped the bully?*), Reinforcer (e.g., *How often have you laughed at people getting bullied?*), Defender (e.g., *How often have you tried to make others stop bullying*), and Bystander (e.g., *How often have you done nothing and just waited until the bullying stopped?*). For each item participants responded using a 3-point scale (0 = never, 1 = sometimes, 2 = often). We found substantial overlap among the first three scales in our sample (Bully, Assistant, Reinforcer; $\alpha = .71$). In addition, a principal component factor analysis revealed that items from these three subscales all loaded onto the same factor. Therefore we collapsed the Bully, Assistant, and Reinforcer subscales into a single *Bully* scale. The *Defender* scale ($\alpha = .79$) and the *Bystander* scale ($\alpha = .65$) showed adequate internal reliability as well.

A confirmatory factor analysis was then conducted on the three-factor solution (Joining in bullying, Defending, Bystander). The fit of this model was adequate, $\chi^2(df = 116) = 255.59$, CFI = .902, RMSEA = .052.

RESULTS

Descriptive information

Table 1 presents the range, mean, and standard deviation for all study variables.

Is there evidence of PI in the context of witnessed bullying episodes?

In order to address this question, as well as to examine potential age and gender effects, we used a mixed-model ANOVA with attitude as a repeated measure ("me" versus "them"), and gender and grade as between-group measures. Recall that higher scores on "me" and "them" measures indicate more prosocial attitudes (e.g., greater disapproval of bulling, greater empathy for the victim, and more respect for defending behaviors). A bivariate correlation indicated that "me" and "them" were moderately correlated with each other, $r(444) = .47$, $p < .001$. Results of the ANOVA revealed a significant effect of attitude, $F(1, 437) = 274.06$, $p < .01$, $\eta^2 = .39$. Overall, participants reported described their "me" attitudes as more prosocial ($M = 3.36$, $SE = .02$) than their perceived "them" attitudes ($M = 3.00$, $SE = .02$). There was a significant main effect of grade, $F(1, 437) = 66.20$, $p < .001$, $\eta^2 = .13$. Fourth graders reported more prosocial attitudes collapsed across "me" and "them" ($M = 3.32$, $SE = .03$) than eighth graders ($M = 3.04$, $SE = .02$). There was also a significant main effect of gender, $F(1, 437) = 5.97$, $p < .05$, $\eta^2 = .01$. Females reported more prosocial attitudes collapsed across "me" and "them" ($M = 3.22$, $SE = .02$) than males ($M = 3.14$, $SE = .02$).

These main effects were qualified by two interactions. As depicted in Figure 1, the significant attitude by gender interaction indicated that while both males and females viewed their own attitudes as more prosocial than their peers' attitudes, this discrepancy was bigger among females. In addition, girls described their "me" attitudes as significantly more prosocial than did males, although there were no gender differences in "them" attitudes, $F(1, 437) = 14.59$, $p < .01$, $\eta^2 = .03$. Finally, there was an attitude by grade interaction, $F(1, 437) = 3.55$, $p = .06$, $\eta^2 = .01$. Both fourth and eighth graders viewed their own attitudes as more prosocial than their peers' attitudes, although the discrepancy was slightly bigger among eighth graders. Fourth graders reported more prosocial attitudes than eighth

TABLE 1
Descriptive information for "me" and "them" attitudes

	Fourth grade		*Eighth grade*	
	Min-Max; M (SD) *Boys*	*Min-Max; M (SD)* *Girls*	*Min-Max; M (SD)* *Boys*	*Min - Max; M (SD)* *Girls*
"Me" attitudes	2.10 to 4; 3.40 (.41)	2.67 to 4; 3.56 (.34)	1.5 to 4; 3.15 (.51)	2.30 to 4; 3.33 (.40)
"Them" attitudes	2.40 to 4; 3.15 (.37)	2.10 to 4; 3.17 (.42)	1.4 to 4; 2.85 (.46)	1.80 to 3.80; 2.83 (.38)
Norm misperception	−0.61 to 1.01; .33 (.36)	−0.49 to 1.41; .32 (.41)	−0.76 to 1.71; .36 (.43)	−0.46 to 1.44; .44 (.39)
Joining in the bullying	0 to .67; .11 (.14)	0 to .71; .07 (.11)	0 to 1.78; .29 (.29)	0 to .78; .17 (.19)
Defending the victim	0 to 2.00; 1.19 (.58)	0 to 2.00; 1.35 (.53)	0 to 2.00; 1.09 (.51)	0 to 2.00; 1.01 (.54)
Watching passively	0 to 2.00; .98 (.47)	0 to 2.00; .86 (.46)	0 to 1.80; .98 (.34)	0 to 2; 1.09 (.38)

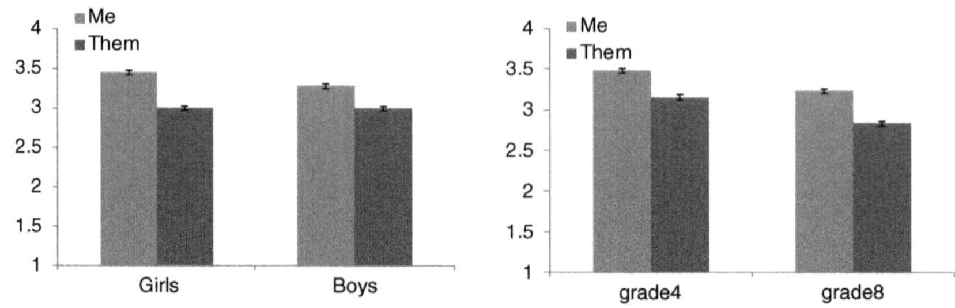

Figure 1. Gender and age effects on "me" and "them" attitudes.

graders for both "me" and "them" attitudes, although the grade difference was slightly bigger for "them" attitudes.

Is there an association between misperceptions of group norms and participant role behavior?

We computed a "norm misperception score" for each child by subtracting that child's perception of the group attitude ("them" score) from the actual mean of the group's responses to the attitude questions (average of all "me" scores for each school). Norm misperception scores ranged from −.76 to 1.71 ($M = .37$, $SD = .40$). A norm misperception score of zero would indicate perfect accuracy in estimating group norms (i.e., a child's estimate of classmates' attitudes was exactly the same as the average "me" attitudes actually reported by their classmates. A positive norm misperception score (i.e. actual attitude of classmates > perceived attitude of classmates) indicated a tendency to underestimate how prosocial the peer group's attitude really was. A negative norm misperception score (actual attitude of classmates < perceived attitude) indicated a tendency to overestimate how prosocial the peer group's attitude really was.

Table 2 depicts the correlations among norm misperception scores and the three behavioral responses to witnessing bullying (initiating or joining in the bullying, watching passively, and defending the victim). Norm misperception was positively associated with joining in with ongoing bullying and negatively associated with actively defending victims, indicating that the more students *underestimated* the extent to which their peers held prosocial attitudes, the more likely they were to support bullies, and the less likely they were to defend victimized classmates.

Using the continuous norm misperception score we created a *categorical* norm misperception score; participants were labeled as underestimators of peers' prosocial attitudes if their norm misperception score was greater than 0, and as overestimators of peers' prosocial attitudes if their norm

TABLE 2
Correlations among norm misperception scores and behavioral responses to witnessed bullying ($N = 441$)

	1	*2*	*3*	*4*
1. Norm misperception		.29**	.04	−.16**
2. Joining in			.02	−.22**
3. Watching passively				−.20**
4. Actively defending				

Positive norm misperception scores indicate a tendency to perceive peers as holding *fewer* prosocial attitudes than they actually do; negative scores indicate a tendency to perceive peers as holding *more* prosoical attitudes than they actually do.
**$p < .01$.

TABLE 3
Frequency of over- and under-estimators of classmates' attitudes as a function of grade and gender

		Grade		
		Fourth	*Eighth*	*Total*
Overestimators of classmates' prosocial attitudes	Males	18	22	40
	Females	19	14	33
	Total	37	36	73
Underestimators of classmates' prosocial attitudes	Males	70	111	181
	Females	68	119	187
	Total	138	230	368

misperception score was less than 0. Table 3 depicts the frequency of under- and over- estimators by grade and gender.

To examine potential associations between misperceptions of group norms and behavior we computed univariate ANOVAs predicting children's responses to witnessed bullying events. We ran separate ANOVAs for each of the three behavioral response measures (Joining in, Actively Defending, Passively Watching). Independent variables included categorical norm misperception score, grade, and gender. In each analysis the two behavioral response measures not serving as the dependent variable were included as covariates.

Joining in the bullying. There was a significant effect of gender on students' reports of joining in the bullying, $F(1, 431) = 9.85$, $p < .01$, $\eta^2 = .02$. Males reported higher levels of joining in ($M = .22$, $SD = .25$)

than females ($M = .13$, $SD = .16$). There was also a significant effect of grade on students' reports of joining in, $F(1, 431) = 16.36$, $p < .001$, $\eta^2 = .04$. Eighth graders reported higher levels of joining in ($M = .23$, $SD = .25$) than fourth graders ($M = .09$, $SD = .12$). Finally, there was a significant effect of norm misperception on students' reports of joining in the bullying, $F(1, 431) = 6.16$, $p < .05$, $\eta^2 = .01$. Students who underestimated the extent to which their classmates held prosocial attitudes reported higher levels of joining in ($M = .19$, $SD = .23$) than students who overestimated the extent to which their classmates held prosocial attitudes ($M = .10$, $SD = .15$).

Actively defending the victim. There were no significant effects of grade or gender on students' reports of actively defending victims. There was, however, a significant effect of norm misperception on students' reports of actively defending, $F(1, 431) = 7.85$, $p < .01$, $\eta^2 = .02$. Students who underestimated the extent to which their classmates held prosocial attitudes reported lower levels of defending ($M = 1.10$, $SD = .54$) than students who overestimated the extent to which their classmates held prosocial attitudes ($M = 1.37$, $SD = .51$).

Passively watching. There were no significant effects of grade, gender, or norm misperception on students' reports of passively standing by and watching when they witnessed bullying episodes.

DISCUSSION

The ultimate concern of this study was to explore differences in children's responses to witnessed bullying. We focused on pluralistic ignorance (PI) and norm misperception as potential explanations for constrained helping behavior. Our first goal in the current study was to apply the concept of PI to bystander behavior. To that end we explored whether children systematically perceived their own attitudes about bullies, victims, and defenders as "out of step" with those of their classmates. Next we examined the degree to which individual differences in norm misperception were associated with children's behavioral responses to witnessed incidents of peer harassment. We hypothesized that there would be a significant association between norm misperception and behavior, such that children who underestimated the extent to which the larger group held prosocial attitudes toward bullies and victims would engage in lower levels of active defending and higher levels of passive bystander behavior.

Before addressing our specific hypotheses about PI, it is important to note some key descriptive information about bullying and defending behavior that emerged in our sample. First, our results revealed significant age and gender differences in children's typical behavioral responses to witnessed bullying. Overall, eighth graders reported engaging in more joining in with bullying than fourth graders. This pattern of results is consistent with demographic data from other studies (e.g., Pepler et al., 2006).

We also found a significant main effect of gender on children's responses to witnessed bullying. Across grades, males were more likely to initiate or join in on ongoing bullying than females. These findings are also consistent with existing literature (e.g., Boulton & Underwood, 1992; Cook, Williams, Guerra, Kim, & Sadek, 2010; Lagerspetz, Björkqvist, Berts, & King, 1982; Salmivalli et al., 1996; Whitney & Smith, 1993). In part this gender difference may have something to do with differences in the *manner* in which boys and girls aggress against classmates. Many studies have shown that girls engage in fewer physical forms of bullying than boys, and instead tend to choose *relational* forms of harassment when they target their peers (Crick & Grotpeter, 1995). To the extent that relational forms of aggression are often private, subtle, indirect, and difficult to interpret clearly as hostile, they may be harder to recognize as acts of bullying.

The descriptive information reported here is consistent with prior studies on bullying, providing some reassurance that our data are valid and reliable. With this in mind, we now turn to our primary research questions. Our first research question addressed the extent to which children exhibited PI in the context of witnessing bullying episodes. As predicted, we did find evidence of PI in this domain. When participants were asked to report their own attitudes as well as their perceptions of their peers' attitudes, they viewed themselves as more prosocial than their peers. Also in line with our predictions, we found age and gender effects on children's level of PI in the context of bullying. Females expressed higher levels of PI than males, and eighth graders displayed higher levels of PI than fourth graders.

The gender difference reported here is consistent with prior literature on PI (e.g., Hines et al., 2002; Prentice & Miller, 1993; Sandstrom & Bartini, 2010). The reasons for this gender difference in the context of witnessing bullying are not entirely clear, but it is possible that the stereotypical portrayal of females as more empathic and caring may lead girls to view themselves as especially prosocial relative to their classmates. Boys, on the other hand, might underestimate their prosocial attitudes in an attempt to conform to the cultural stereotype of males as independent, unemotional, and tough. For both males and females, PI appeared to increase with age. We speculate that this increase has to do, in part, with developmental increases in the ability to dissemble by masking private attitudes and emotions (e.g., Saarni, 1988), as well as in the ability to use social comparisons as a means of evaluating the self (e.g., Ruble et al., 1980),

Next we turn our attention to our second research question: Is norm misperception associated with children's typical behavioral responses when they witness bullying episodes at school? We expected children who underestimated the prosocial sentiment of the larger group to engage in *less* defending and *more* bystander behavior, in an attempt to match their behavior to their perceptions of group norms.

Our results provided some support for this hypothesis: while norm misperception was not associated with children's reports of passivity, it was associated with their reports of defending behavior. Children who underestimated the extent to which their peers held prosocial attitudes were less likely to describe themselves as active defenders than children who overestimated. One explanation for this finding is that children use their perceptions of group norms to guide their behavioral responses when they witness the bullying of classmates. Those who "read" the attitude of their peers accurately (or even overestimate their prosocial sentiments) may feel more comfortable stepping up to help victimized peers because they believe the group values such behavior. Helping a victim may feel considerably less scary when potential defenders imagine that their classmates support and admire such actions. In contrast, children who mistakenly view their classmates as more tolerant of bullies or less supportive of potential defenders than they actually are may attempt to conform to the illusory norm by refraining from active defending behavior. In short, *not* defending victimized classmates may feel like a safer and more popular option than defending them (e.g., Pozzoli & Gini, 2010).

Interestingly, norm misperception was also associated with children's tendency to join in or otherwise reinforce ongoing bullying episodes. Children who underestimated the prosocial sentiments of the group were more likely to join in the bullying than those who held overly positive expectations for the group. Again, this finding is consistent with the premise that children may use their perceptions of group attitudes to shape their own behavior. The more they underestimate the group's moral standards, the more likely they may be to join in when they witness peer mistreatment.

Limitations

An important strength of the current study is its application of PI to a new context, and the inclusion of two age groups in order to explore the association between children's perception of group norms and their behavioral responses to witnessed bullying episodes. Nevertheless, several limitations should be noted.

First, the correlational nature of our design leaves the issue of causal direction between norm misperception and behavioral responses to witnessed bullying open to interpretation. Children who underestimate the prosocial attitude of the group may constrain helping behavior or reinforce ongoing bullying behavior in a mistaken attempt to match their behavior to the group norm. On the other hand, it is equally possible that the direction of causality operates in reverse; children's responses to witnessed bullying may shape the accuracy of their perceptions over time. Children who frequently act to defend victims may create an opportunity to receive positive feedback from peers, leading them to develop a perception of their classmates as prosocial. At the same time, children who fail to defend victims might fail to receive any clear feedback, allowing them to maintain the mistaken belief that their peers don't particularly admire or value active helping. In future research, experimental manipulation of children's perceptions of group attitudes may allow us to tease apart these competing explanations more conclusively.

A second limitation involves our reliance on self-report to assess children's response to witnessed bullying. This approach was based on the premise that children may be in the best position to provide information about their own behavior, and was designed explicitly to mitigate concerns associated with teacher-reported behavioral responses reported elsewhere (Sandstrom & Bartini, 2010). Nevertheless, self-report measures carry their own set of limitations. It is possible that the associations between PI and behavior reported here may reflect, in part, children's impression management strategies, preferences for responding to questionnaires, or shared method variance. While some of these concerns issues were mitigated (e.g., we emphasized the confidential nature of the data in order to de-emphasize impression management strivings), they could not be eradicated completely. In future research it will be important to augment both self and teacher ratings with peer nominations and direct behavioral observation of children's responses when they witness peer mistreatment.

A third limitation of the current study was that our operational definitions of PI and norm misperception involved children's perceptions of peers in general. It is clear, however, that different social groups within the same classroom can have varying norms about bullying (e.g., Duffy & Nesdale, 2009). Further, researchers who study PI in the context of college drinking have found that students' attitudes about their own *friends* are more potent predictors of their behavior than attitudes about college students in general (e.g., LaBrie, Hummer, Neighbors, & Larimer, 2010). We might have found different results if we had asked children to report on the attitudes of their friends or of the popular crowd, rather than classmates at large.

Finally, it is important to realize that passivity in the face of witnessed bullying is a complex problem, and that misperception of group norms is only one of a myriad potential contributing factors. Indeed, passivity may be shaped by processes occurring at multiple levels of influence. Individual traits, such as fear of retaliation, self-efficacy, self-esteem, resistance to peer influence, status, and skill at defending each play an important role (e.g., Boden, Fergusson, & Horwood, 2007; Gini et al. 2008; Mishna & Alaggia, 2005; Poyhonen et al., 2010; Pozzoli & Gini, 2010; Salmivalli et al., 1999; Sentse et al., 2007).

Further, a variety of interpersonal factors may act to shape children's responses when they witness bullying. It is possible, for instance, that children may hold a general belief that bullying is wrong, but feel less inclined to intervene in specific incidents because they have an affinity with a particular bully, or distaste for a particular victim. Finally, larger cultural influences may serve to constrain helping behavior as well. Perhaps certain Western values (e.g., *I should act in my own best interest*; *People should be responsible for themselves*; *What is in it for me?*) encourage children to remain passive in the face of bullying. Future research will need to explore these other factors more closely.

Implications and future directions

If future research does support a causal role for norm misperception in the constraint of active defending behavior, it could have novel implications for school-based bully prevention programs. Many intervention programs are geared toward changing school climate by targeting bystanders' *personal* attitudes about bullies and victims (i.e., encouraging a desire or impulse to help victimized classmates), and by teaching them a set of behavioral skills for *how* to intervene (i.e., learning what to say to a bully or when to get the support of an adult). Such programs are in widespread use across the country (e.g., *Steps to Respect*; Frey et al., 2005; *Bully Busters*; Horne, Bartolomucci & Newman-Carlson, 2003; *Olweus Bullying Prevention Program*; Olweus, Limber & Mihalic, 1999).

Perhaps an additional way to tackle bullying is to focus on revealing children's erroneous assumptions about the attitudes of their peers. There is growing evidence in the alcohol literature that experimental manipulation of individuals' knowledge of group norms can result in changed behavior (e.g., LaBrie et al., 2008; Schroeder & Prentice, 1998). In the case of school bullying we hypothesize that providing concrete information about how mistakes in norm estimation arise (i.e., *Sometimes your classmates have private beliefs that don't match their public behaviors*), as well as offering accurate and specific information about real norms in the classroom (i.e., *Nine out of ten students at your school believe that helping a victim is the right thing to do*), would give students a more clear view of shared norms among their classmates. This public "unmasking" of misperceived norms could, in turn, empower students to stand together to create a safer and more tolerant school community.

REFERENCES

Aiken, L. S., & West, S. G. (1991). *Multiple regression: Testing and interpreting interactions*. Thousand Oaks, CA: Sage Publications, Inc.

Belacchi, C. (2008). Participant roles in bullying: A new proposal. *Giornale Italiano di Psicologia, 4*, 885–912.

Boden, J., Fergusson, D., & Horwood, L. (2007). Self-esteem and violence: Testing links between adolescent self-esteem and later hostility and violent behavior. *Social Psychiatry and Psychiatric Epidemiology, 42*, 881–891.

Boulton, M., Bucci, E., & Hawker, D. (1999). Swedish and English secondary school pupils' attitudes towards, and conceptions of, bullying: Concurrent links with bully/victim involvement. *Scandinavian Journal of Psychology, 40*, 277–284.

Boulton, M., & Underwood, K. (1992). Bully/victim problems among middle school children. *British Journal of Educational Psychology, 62*, 73–87.

Charach, A., Pepler, D., & Ziegler, S. (1995). Bullying at school. *Education Canada, 37*, 12–18.

Cook, C. R., Williams, K. R., Guerra, N. G., Kim, T. E., & Sadek, S. (2010). Predictors of bullying and victimization in childhood and adolescence: A meta-analytic investigation. *School Psychology Quarterly, 25*, 65–83.

Crick, N., & Grotpeter, J. (1995). Relational aggression, gender, and social-psychological adjustment. *Child Development, 66*, 710–722.

Duffy, A., & Nesdale, D. (2009). Peer groups, social identity, and children's bullying behavior. *Social Development, 18*, 121–139.

Eslea, M., & Smith, P. (2000). Pupil and parent attitudes towards bullying in primary schools. *European Journal of Psychology of Education, 15*, 207–219.

Frey, K. S., Hirschstein, M. K., Snell, J. L., Edstron, L. V. S., MacKenzie, E. P., & Broderick, C. J. (2005). Reducing playground bullying and supporting beliefs: An experimental trial of the Steps to Respect program. *Developmental Psychology, 41*, 479–491.

Gini, G., Albiero, P., Benelli, B., & Altoe, G. (2008). Determinants of adolescents' active defending and passive bystanding behavior in bullying. *Journal of Adolescence, 31*, 93–105.

Gini, G., Pozzoli, T., Borghi, F., & Franzoni, L. (2008). The role of bystanders in students' perception of bullying and sense of safety. *Journal of School Psychology, 46*, 617–638.

Hawkins, D., Pepler, D., & Craig, W. (2001). Naturalistic observations of peer interventions in bullying. *Social Development, 10*, 512–527.

Hines, D., Saris, R., & Throckmorton-Belzer, L. (2002). Pluralistic ignorance and health risk behaviors: Do college students misperceive social approval for risky behaviors on campus and in media. *Journal of Applied Social Psychology, 32*, 2621–2640.

Horne, A. M., Bartolomucci, C. L., & Newman-Carlson, D. (2003). *Bully busters: A teacher's manual for helping bullies, victims, and bystanders (grades K-5)*. Champaign, IL: Research Press.

Hymel, S., Rocke-Henderson, N., & Bonanno, R. A. (2005). Moral disengagement: A framework for understanding bullying among adolescents. *Journal of Social Sciences Special Issue, 8*, 1–11.

Hymel, S., Schonert-Reichl, K. A., Bonanno, R. A., Vaillancourt, T., & Rocke Henderson, N. (2010). Bully and morality: Understanding how good kids can behave badly. In S. R. Jimerson, S. M. Swearer, & D. L. Espelage (Eds.), *Handbook of bullying in schools: An international perspective* (pp. 101–118). New York: Routledge.

LaBrie, J., Hummer, J., Neighbors, C., & Larimer, M. (2010). Whose opinion matters? The relationship between injunctive norms and alcohol consequences in college students. *Addictive Behaviors, 35*, 343–349.

LaBrie, J., Hummer, J. F., Neighbors, C., & Pedersen, E. R. (2008). Live interactive group-specific normative feedback reduces misperceptions and drinking in college students: A randomized cluster trial. *Psychology of Addictive Behaviors, 22*, 141–148.

LaBrie, J. W., Hummer, J. F., Grant, S., & Lac, A. (2010). Immediate reductions in misperceived social norms among high-risk college student groups. *Addictive Behaviors, 35*, 1094–1101.

Lagerspetz, K., Björkqvist, K., Berts, M., & King, E. (1982). Group aggression among school children in three schools. *Scandinavian Journal of Psychology, 23*, 45–52.

Menesini, E., Eslea, M., Smith, P. K., Genta, M. L., Giannettti, E., Fonzi, A., et al. (1997). Cross-national comparison of children's attitudes towards bully/victim problems in schools. *Aggressive Behavior, 23*, 245–257.

Miller, D., & McFarland, C. (1991). *When social comparison goes awry: The case of pluralistic ignorance. Social comparison: Contemporary theory and research* (pp. 287–313). Hillsdale, NJ: Lawrence Erlbaum Associates Inc.

Mishna, F., & Alaggia, R. (2005). Weighing the risks: A child's decision to disclose peer victimization. *Children & Schools, 27*, 217–226.

Nesdale, D., Durkin, K., Maass, A., Kiesner, J., & Griffiths, J. (2008). Effects of group norms on children's intentions to bully. *Social Development, 17*, 889–907.

Obermann, M. (2011). Moral disengagement among bystanders to school bullying. *Journal of School Violence, 10*, 239–257.

O'Connell, P., Pepler, D., & Craig, W. (1999). Peer involvement in bullying: Insights and challenges for intervention. *Journal of Adolescence, 22*, 437–452.

Olweus, D., & Limber, S. (2007). *Olweus Bullying Prevention Program: Schoolwide Guide*. Center City Philadelphia: Hazelden.

Olweus, D., Limber, S., & Mihalic, S. (1999). *The Bullying Prevention Program: Blueprints for violence prevention*. Boulder, CO: Center for the Study and Prevention of Violence.

Pellegrini, A. D., & Bartini, M. (2000). An empirical comparison of methods of sampling aggression and vicitimization in school settings. *Journal of Educational Psychology, 92*, 360–366.

Pepler, D., Craig, W., Connolly, J., Yuile, A., McMaster, L., & Jiang, D. (2006). A developmental perspective on bullying. *Aggressive Behavior, 32*, 376–384.

Poyhonen, V., Juvonen, J., & Salmivalli, C. (2010). What does it take to stand up for the victim of bullying? *Merrill Palmer Quarterly, 56*, 143–163.

Pozzoli, T., & Gini, G. (2010). Active defending and passive bystanding behavior in bullying: The role of personal characteristics and perceived peer pressure. *Journal of Abnormal Child Psychology, 38*, 815–827.

Prentice, D., & Miller, D. (1993). Pluralistic ignorance and alcohol use on campus: Some consequences of misperceiving the social norm. *Journal of Personality and Social Psychology*, *64*, 243–256.

Rigby, K., & Slee, P. (1993). Children's attitudes toward victims. In D. Tattum (Ed.), *Understanding and managing bullying* (pp. 119–135). Oxford, UK: Heinemann School Management.

Ruble, D. N., Boggiano, A. K., Feldman, N. S., & Loebl, J. M. (1980). A developmental analysis of the role of social comparison in self-evaluation. *Developmental Psychology*, *16*, 105–115.

Saarni, C. (1988). Children's understanding of the interpersonal consequences of dissemblance of nonverbal emotional-expressive behavior. *Journal of Nonverbal Behavior*, *12*(4), 275–294.

Salmivalli, C., Kaukiainen, A., Kaistaniemi, L., & Lagerspetz, K. (1999). Self-evaluated self-esteem, peer-evaluated self-esteem, and defensive egotism as predictors of adolescents' participation in bullying situations. *Personality and Social Psychology Bulletin*, *25*, 1268–1278.

Salmivalli, C., Lagerspetz, K., Björkqvist, K., Österman, K., & Kaukianen, A. (1996). Bullying as a group process: Participant roles and their relations to social status within the group. *Aggressive Behavior*, *22*, 1–15.

Salmivalli, C., & Voeten, M. (2004). Connections between attitudes, group norms, and behaviour in bullying situations. *International Journal of Behavioral Development*, *28*, 246–258.

Sandstrom, M. J., & Bartini, M. (2010). Do perceptions of discrepancy between self and group norms contribute to peer harassment at school. *Basic and Applied Social Psychology*, *32*, 217–225.

Schroeder, C. M., & Prentice, D. A. (1998). Exposing pluralistic ignorance to reduce alcohol use among college students. *Journal of Applied Social Psychology*, *28*, 2150–2180.

Sentse, M., Scholte, R., Salmivalli, C., & Voeten, M. (2007). Person-group dissimilarity in involvement in bullying and its relation with social status. *Journal of Abnormal Child Psychology*, *35*, 1009–1019.

Shelton, J. N., & Richeson, J. A. (2005). Intergroup contact and pluralistic ignorance. *Journal of Personality & Social Psychology*, *88*, 91–107.

Swearer, S. M., Espelage, D. L, Vaillancourt, T., & Hymel, S. (2010). What can be done about school bullying? Linking research to education practice. *Educational Researcher*, *39*, 38–47.

Twemlow, S. W., Fonagy, P., & Sacco, F. C. (2010). The etiological cast to the role of the bystander in the social architecture of bullying and violence in schools and communities. In S. R. Jimerson, S. M. Swearer, & D. L. Espelage (Eds.), *Handbook of bullying in schools: An international perspective* (pp. 73–86). New York: Routledge.

Van Boven, L. (2000). Pluralistic ignorance and political correctness: The case of affirmative action. *Political Psychology*, *21*, 267–276.

Whitney, I., & Smith, P. (1993). A survey of the nature and extent of bullying in junior/middle and secondary schools. *Educational Research*, *35*, 3–25.

Index

Entries in *italics* refer to figures; entries in **bold** refer to tables.

For Product Safety Concerns and Information please contact our EU representative GPSR@taylorandfrancis.com Taylor & Francis Verlag GmbH, Kaufingerstraße 24, 80331 München, Germany

Batch number: 10726294

Printed by Printforce, the Netherlands